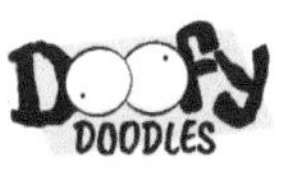

DRAW 25 FARM ANIMALS BADLY

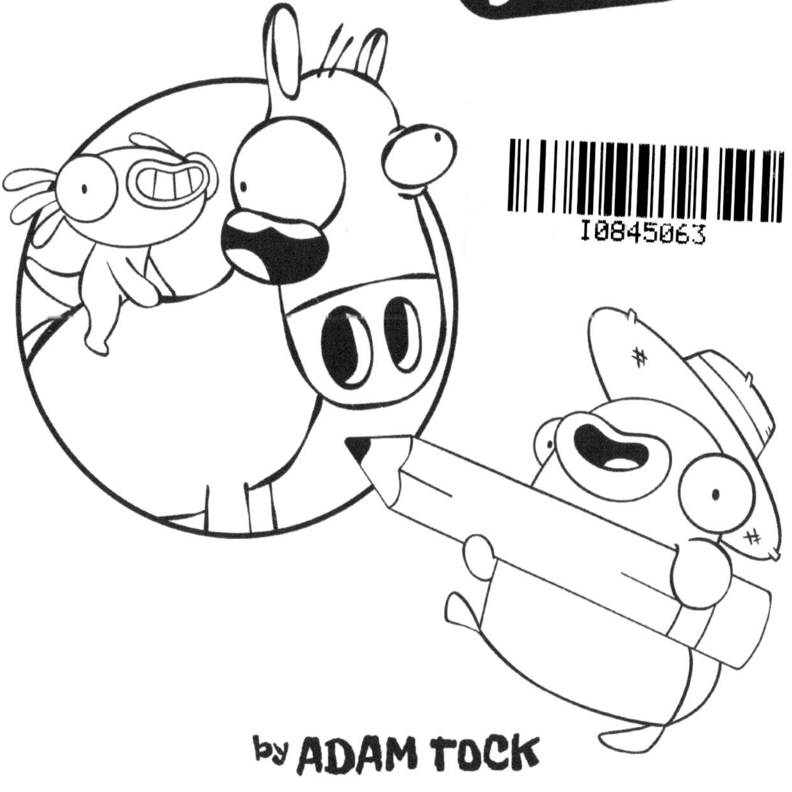

I0845063

by ADAM TOCK

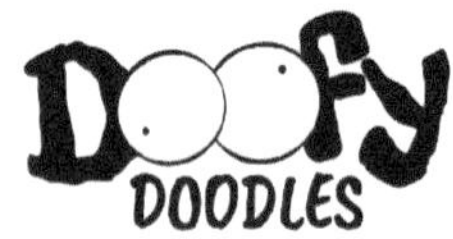

Obscure & Company LLC
1839 Winnetka Ave.
Northfield, IL 60093
https://www.obscureandco.com

ISBN: 979-8-9857620-6-8

Printed in the United States of America
First Edition

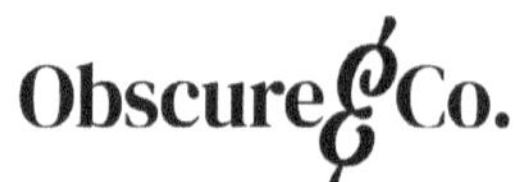

TABLE OF CONTENTS

How to use this book

1. Grab a pencil and eraser.

2. Using the canvas on the right page of every animal, draw each of the steps LIGHTLY in order from 1 to 6 (Step 1 has already been started for you).

3. After you've finished step 5, erase all of your scratch lines to match the final drawing in step 6.

4. Take your drawing a little further by outlining it with pen, marker, or muddy earthworm.

5. Now can you do it WITHOUT the starter shapes?

—or—

Ignore everything we've just told you and do it however you want. This is art, after all!

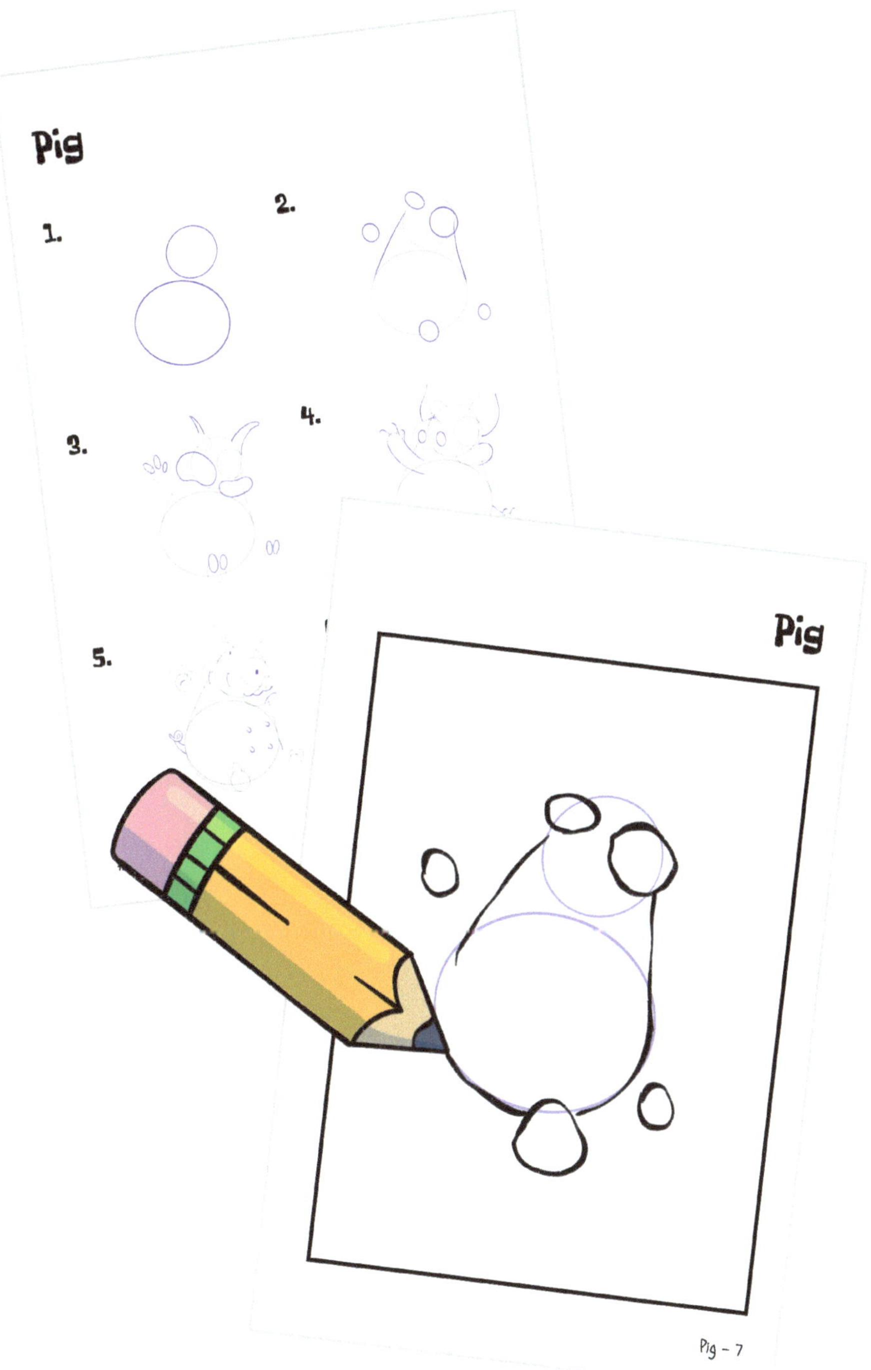
Pig
1.
2.
3.
4.
5.
Pig
Pig - 7

Pig

1.

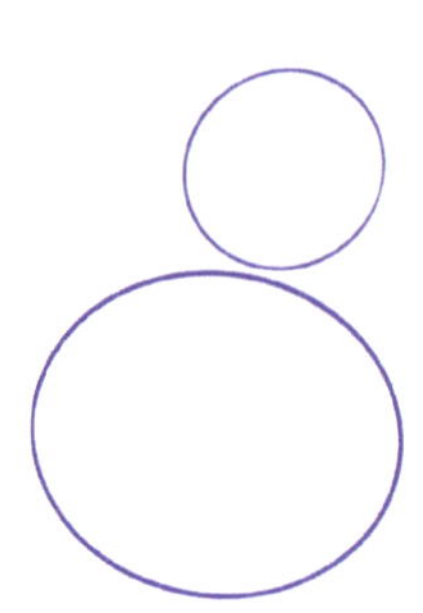

2.

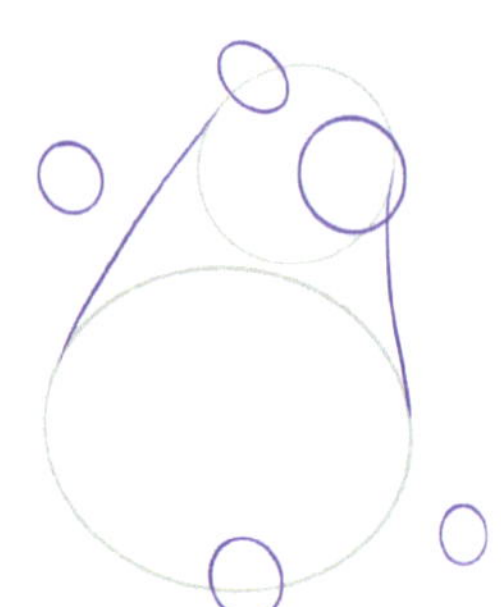

3.

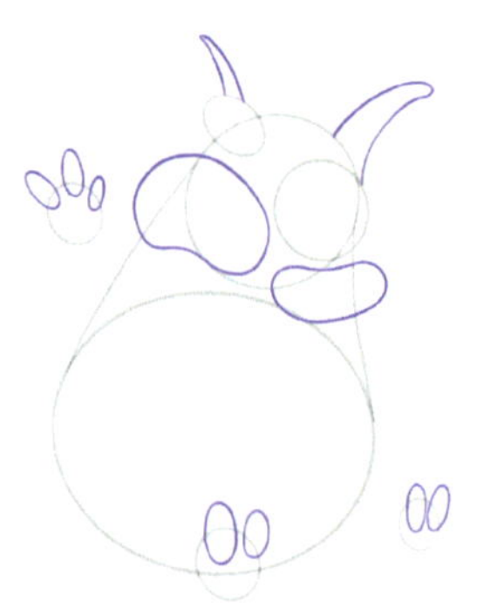

4.

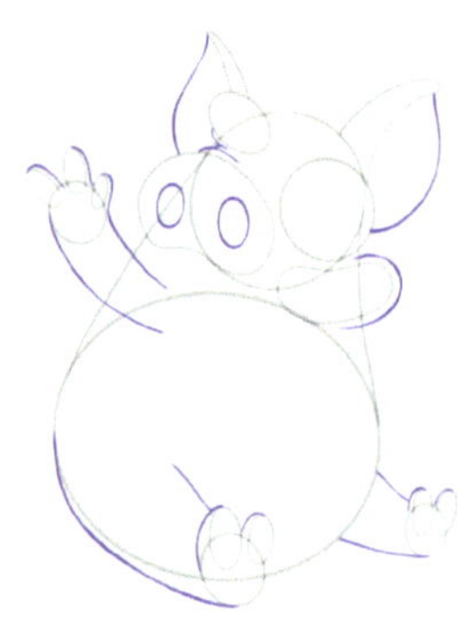

5.

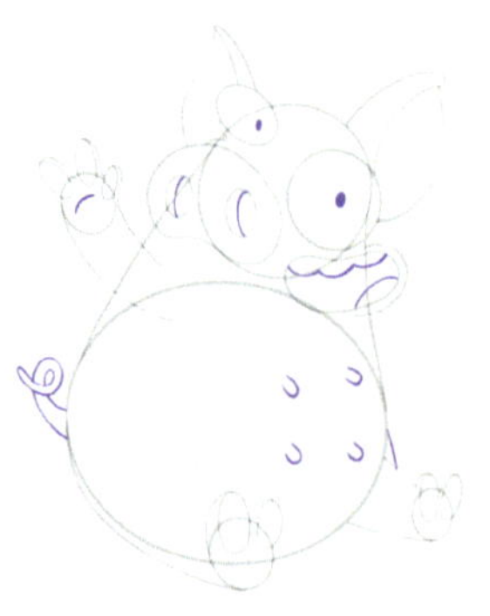

6.

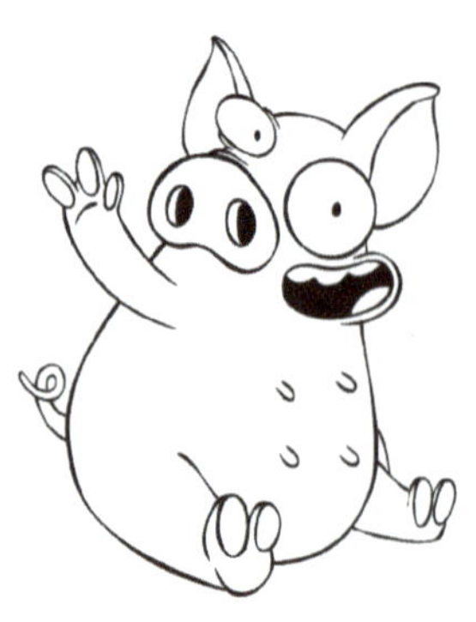

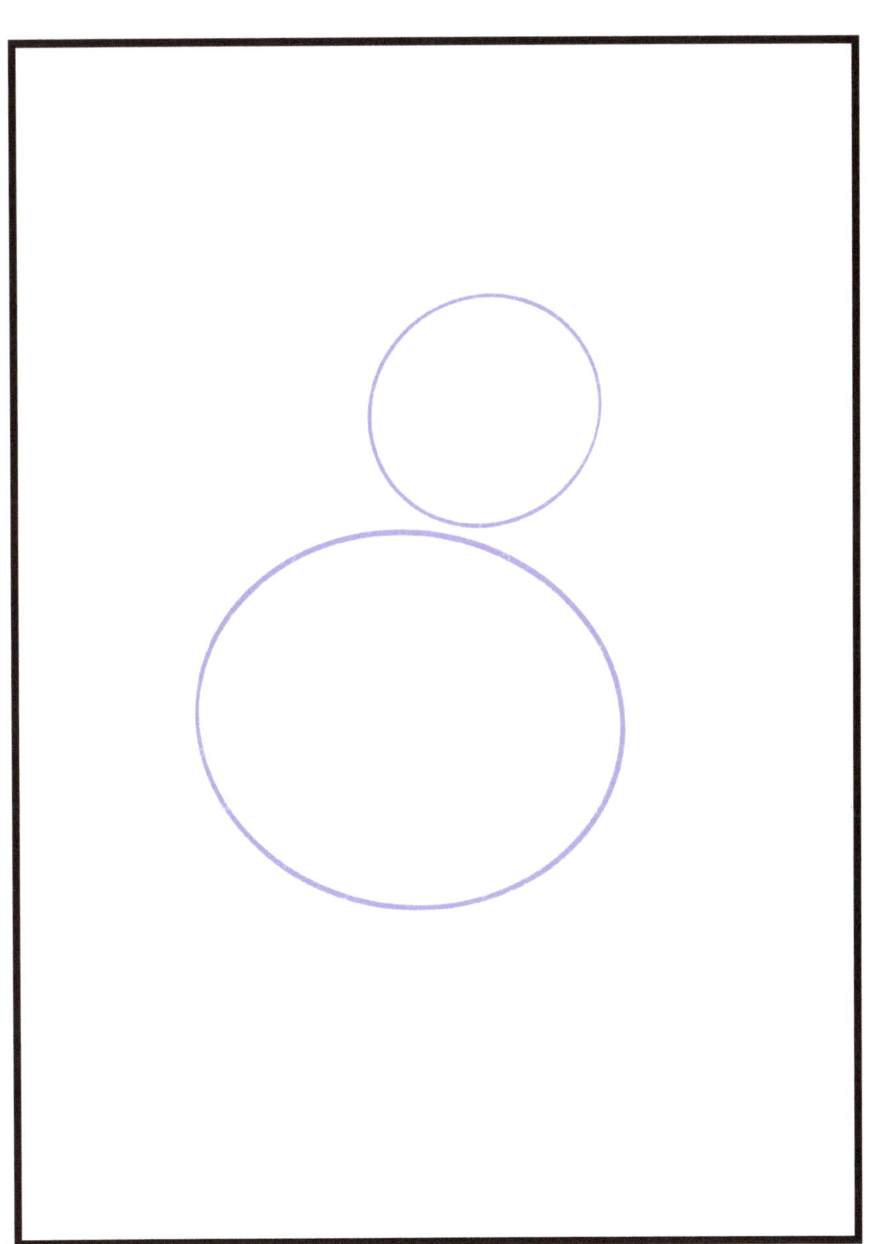

Rooster

1. 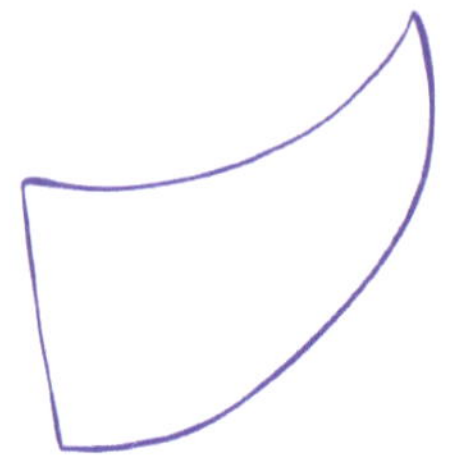

2. 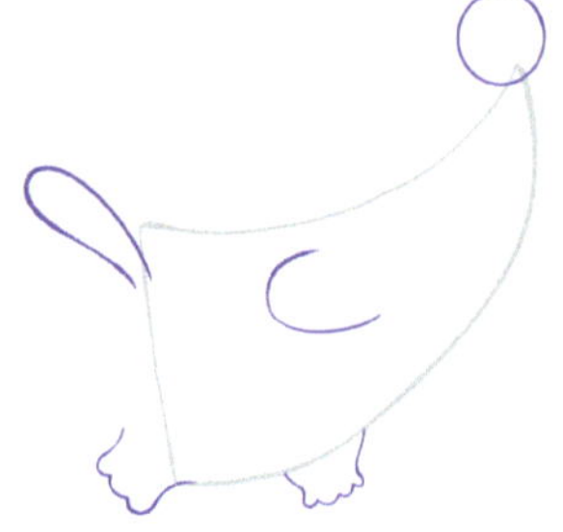

3. 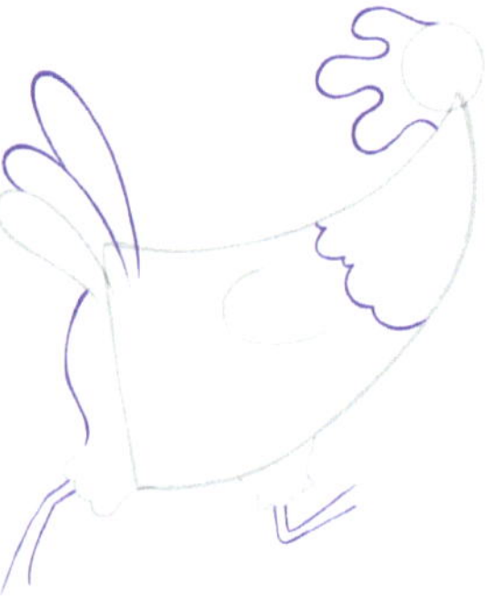

4. 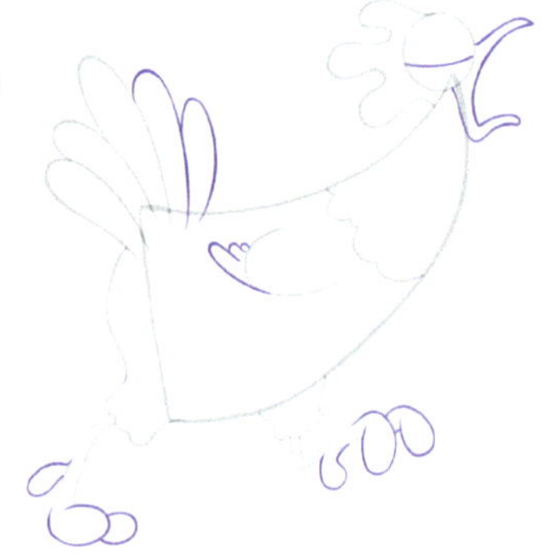

5. 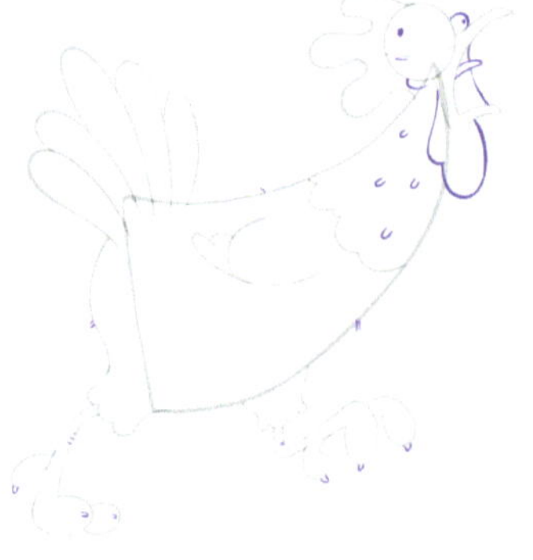

6. 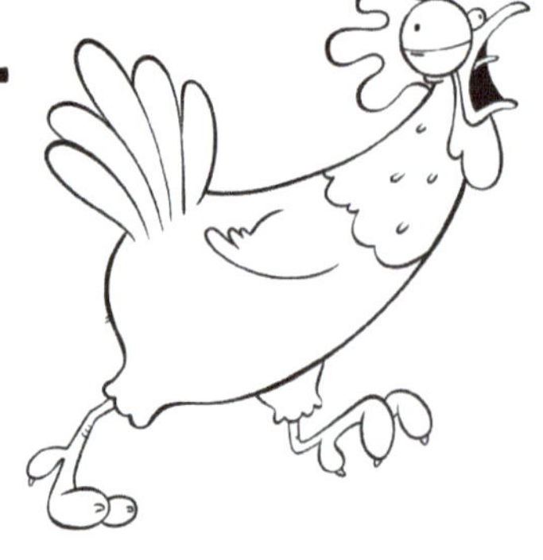

Rooster

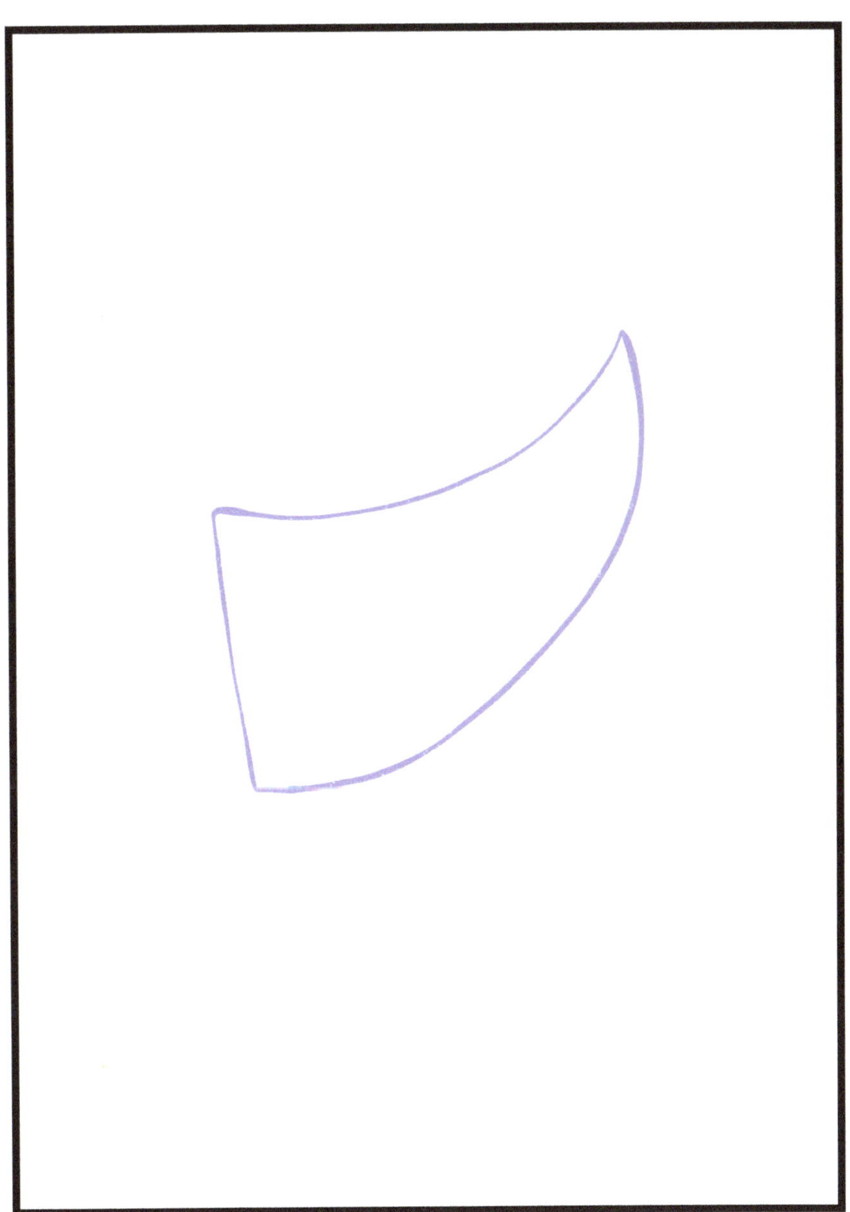

Chicken

1.

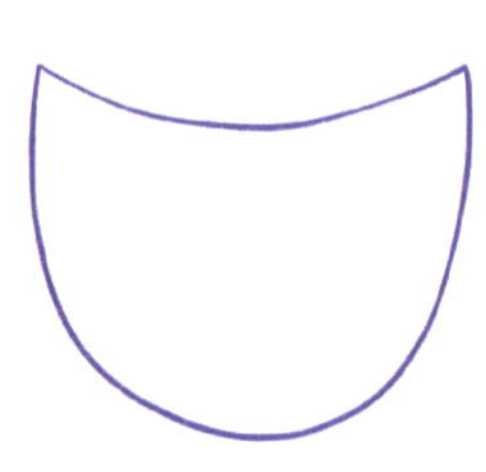

2.

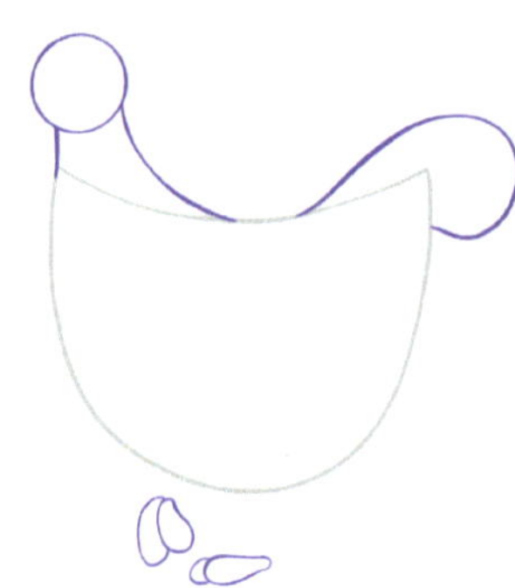

3.

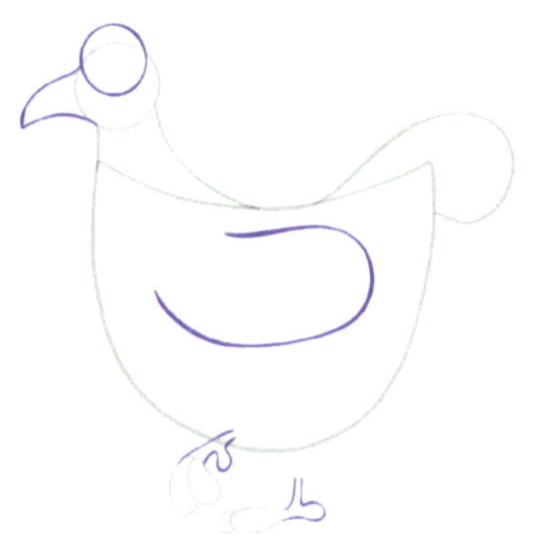

4.

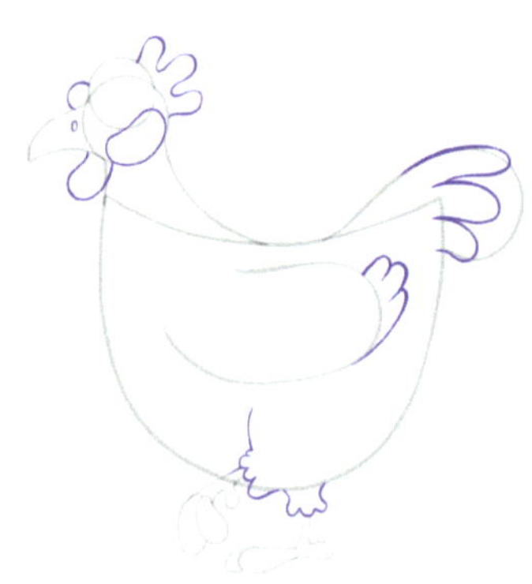

5.

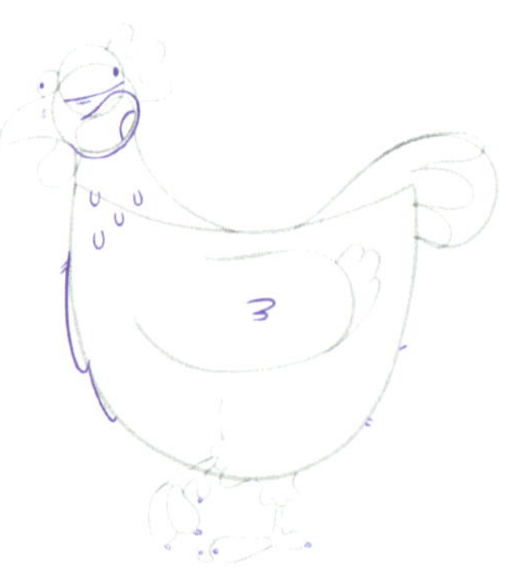

6.

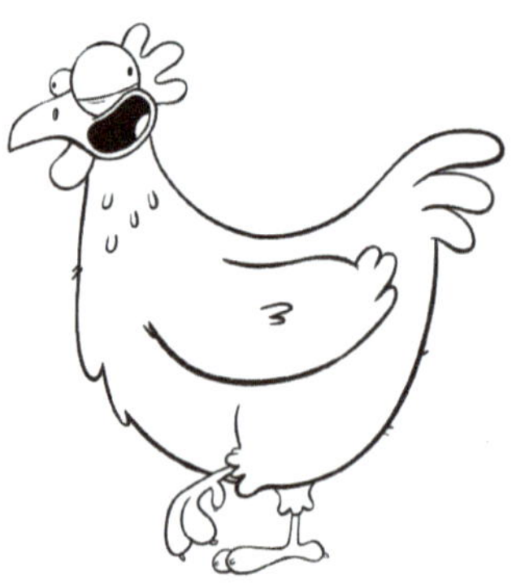

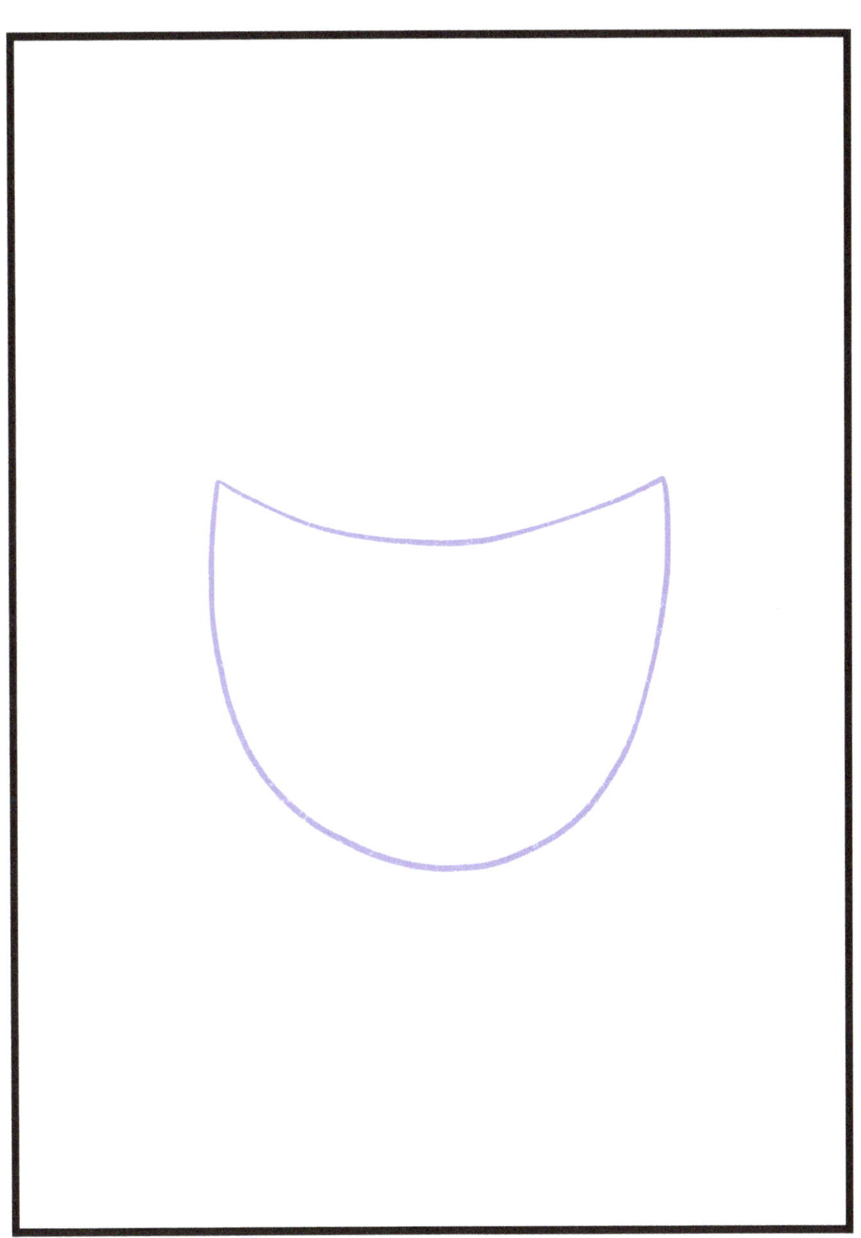

Chick

1. 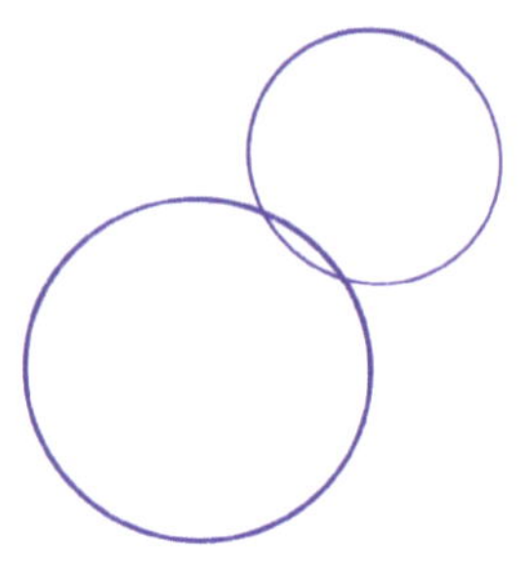

2. 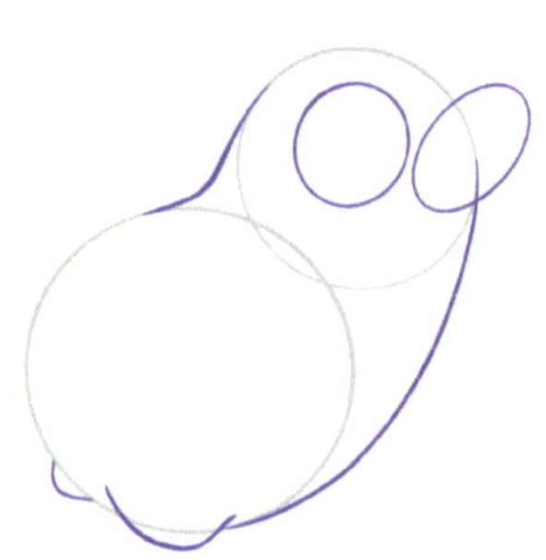

3. 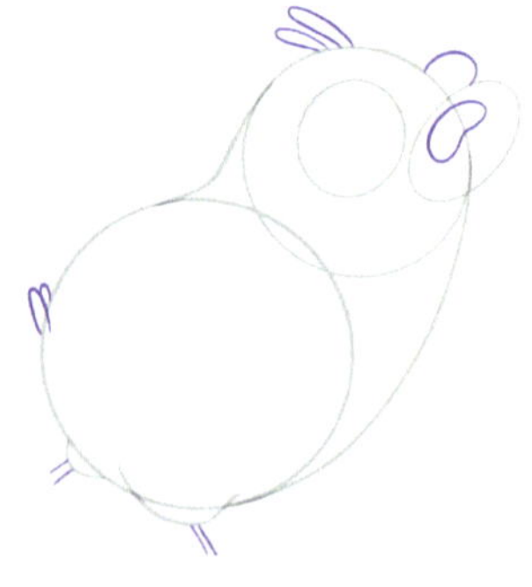

4. 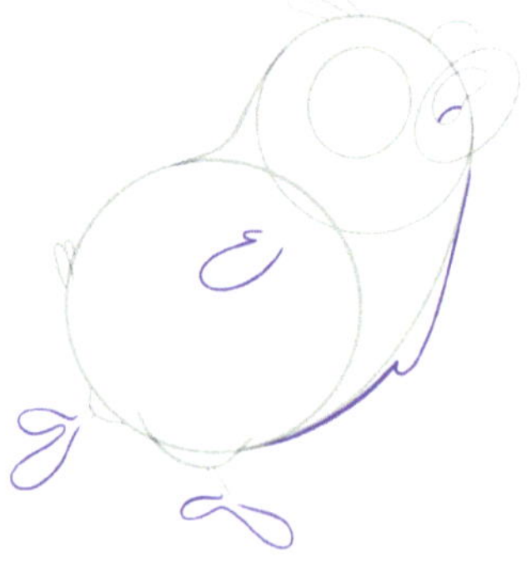

5. 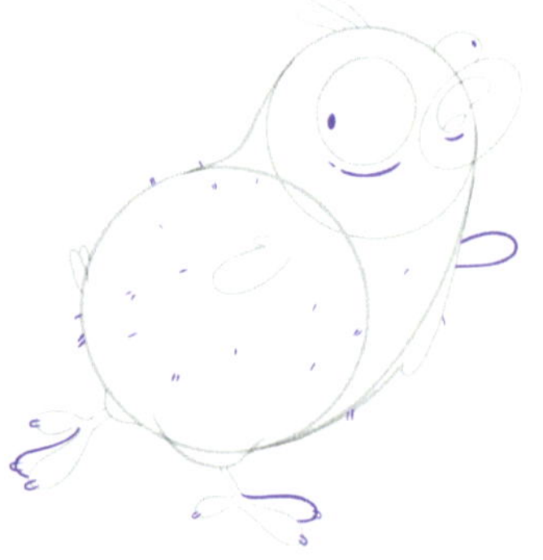

6. 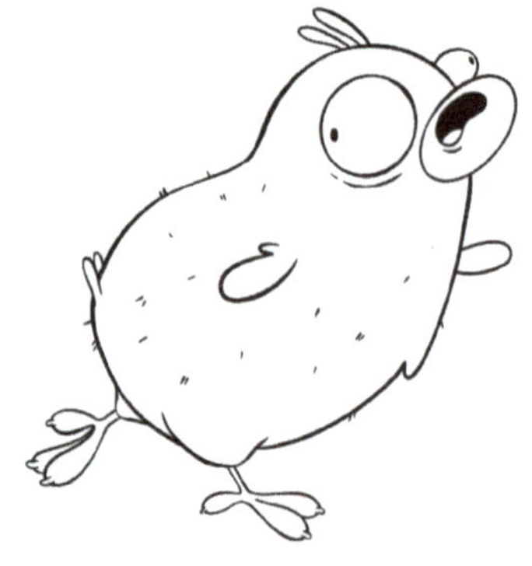

12 – Chick

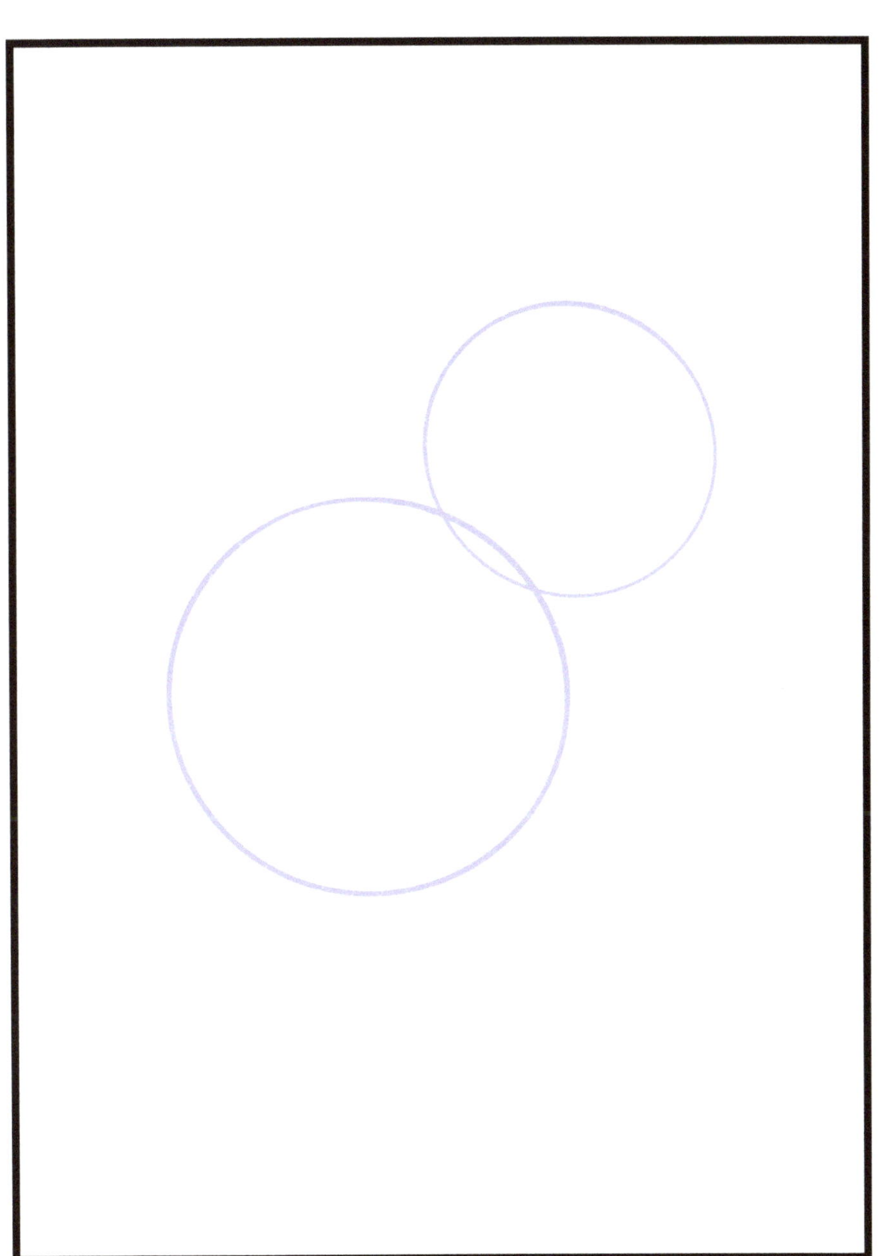

Bull

1. 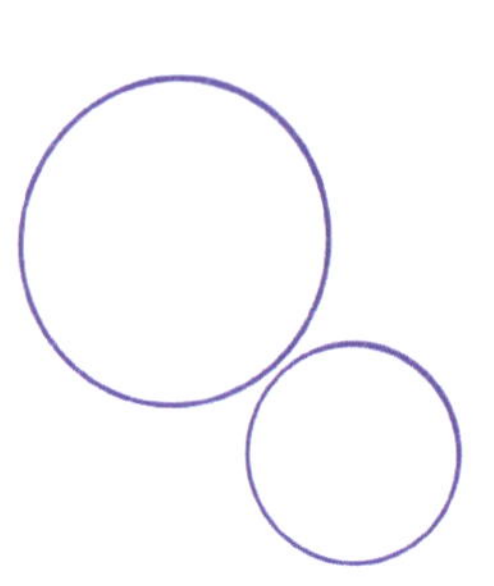

2. 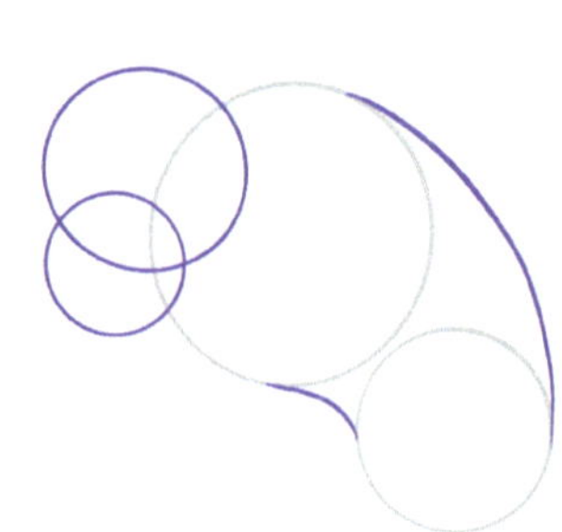

3. 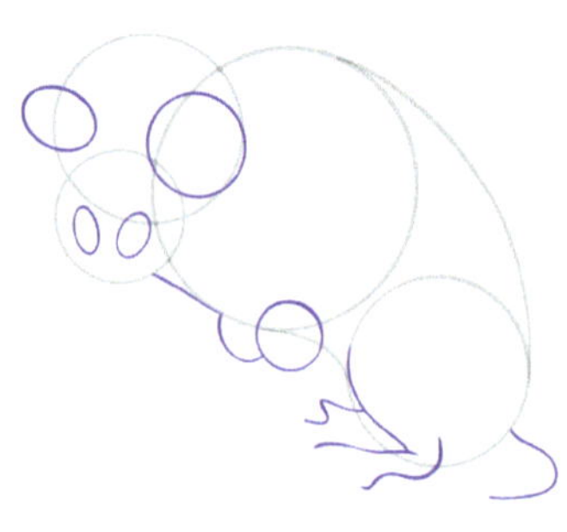

4. 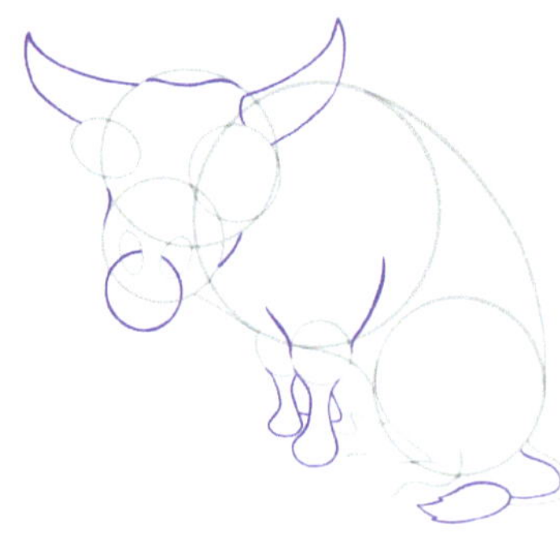

5. 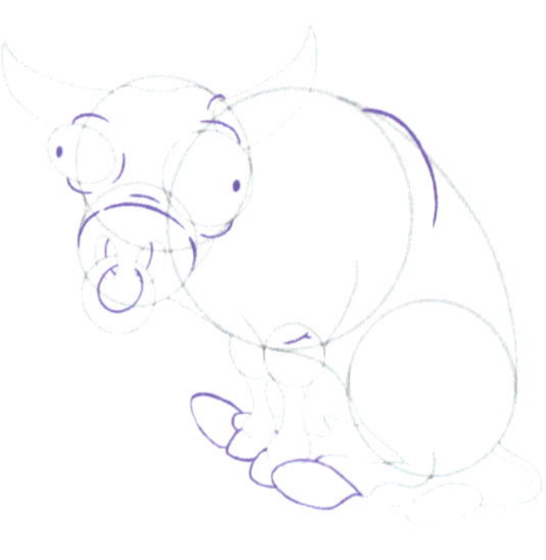

6. 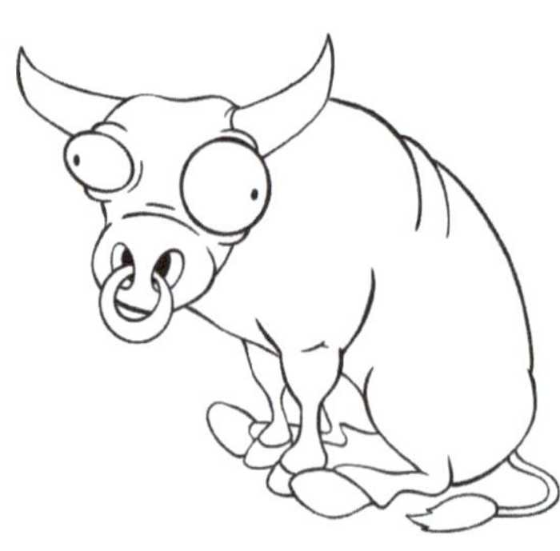

14 – Bull

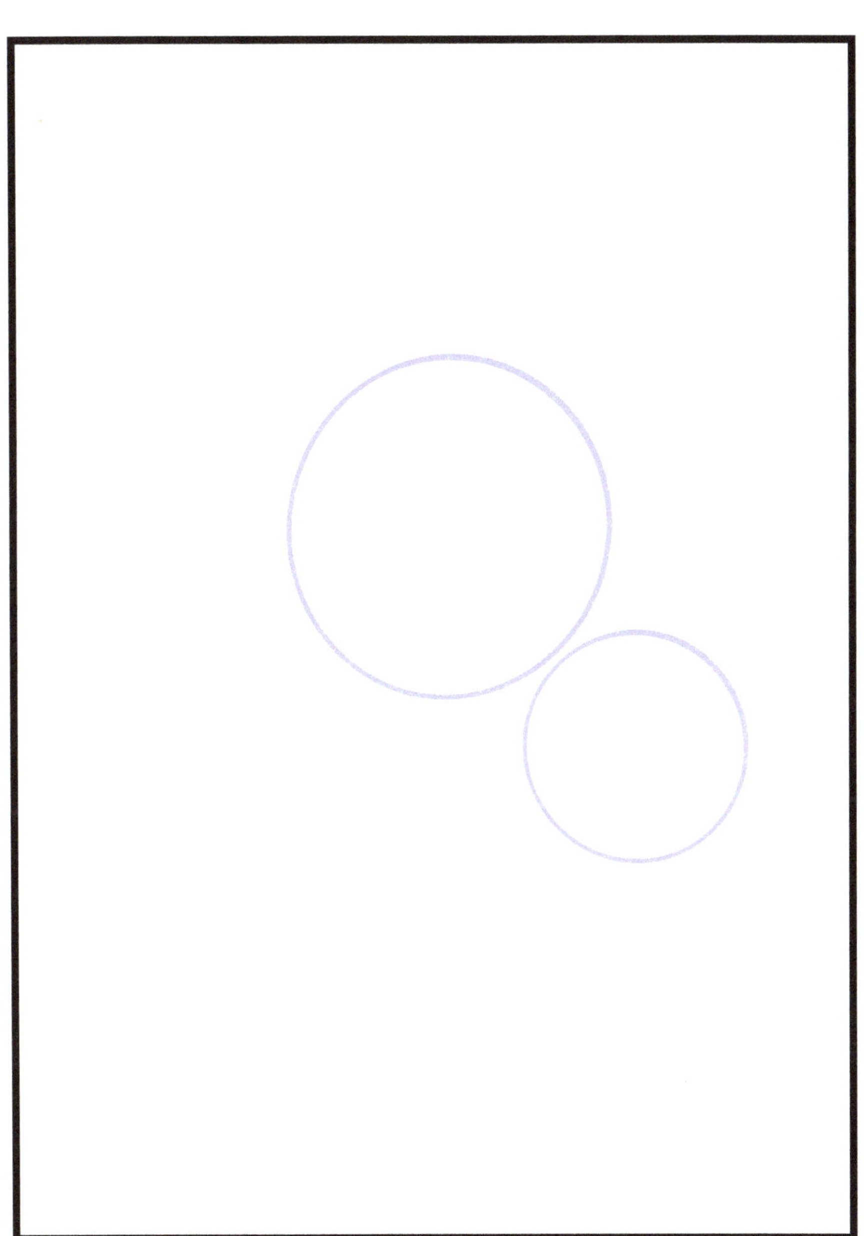

Cow

1.

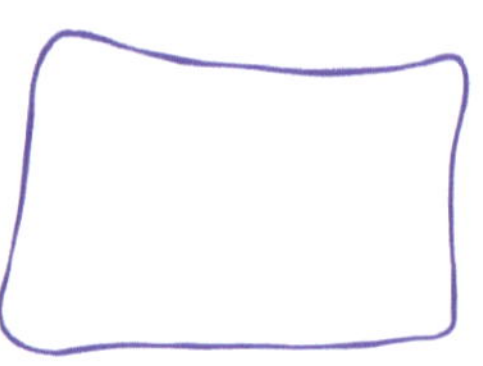

2.

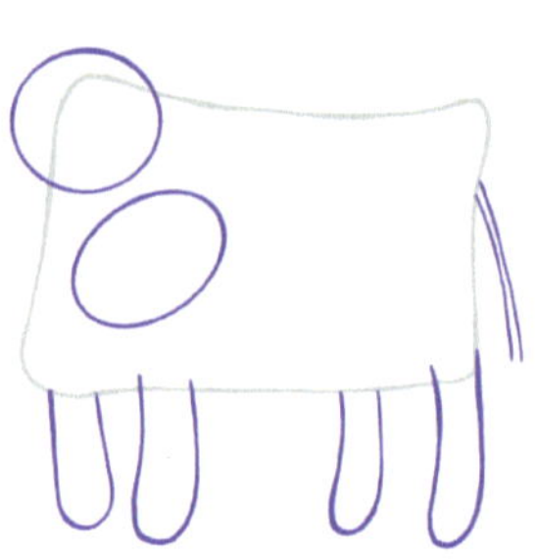

3.

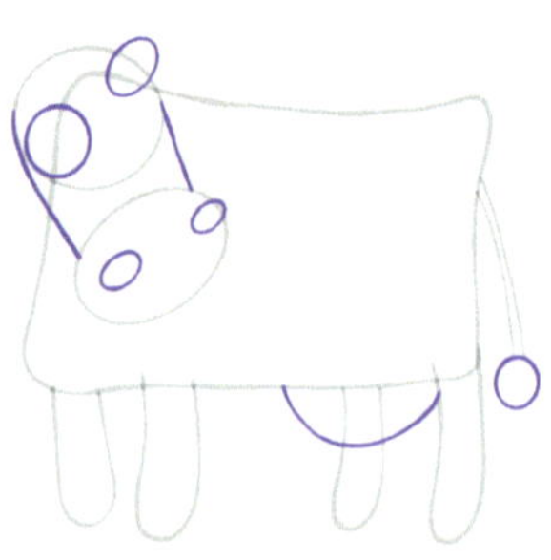

4.

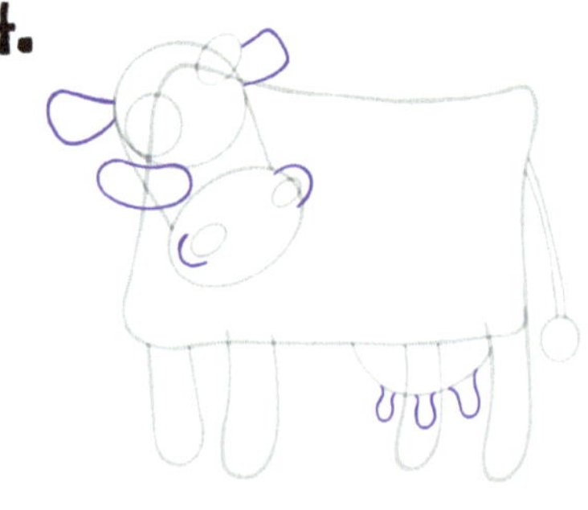

5.

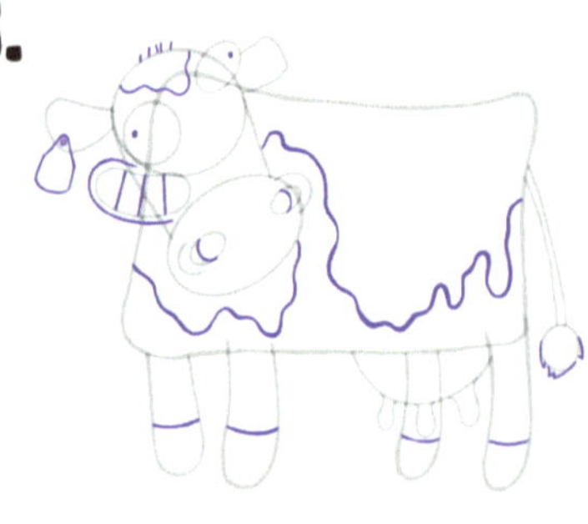

6.

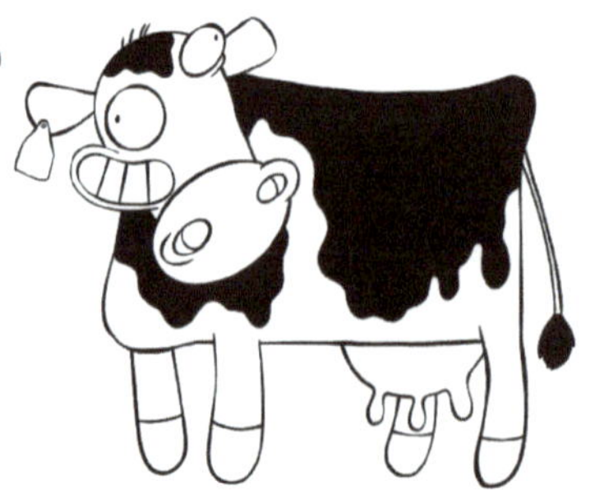

Cow

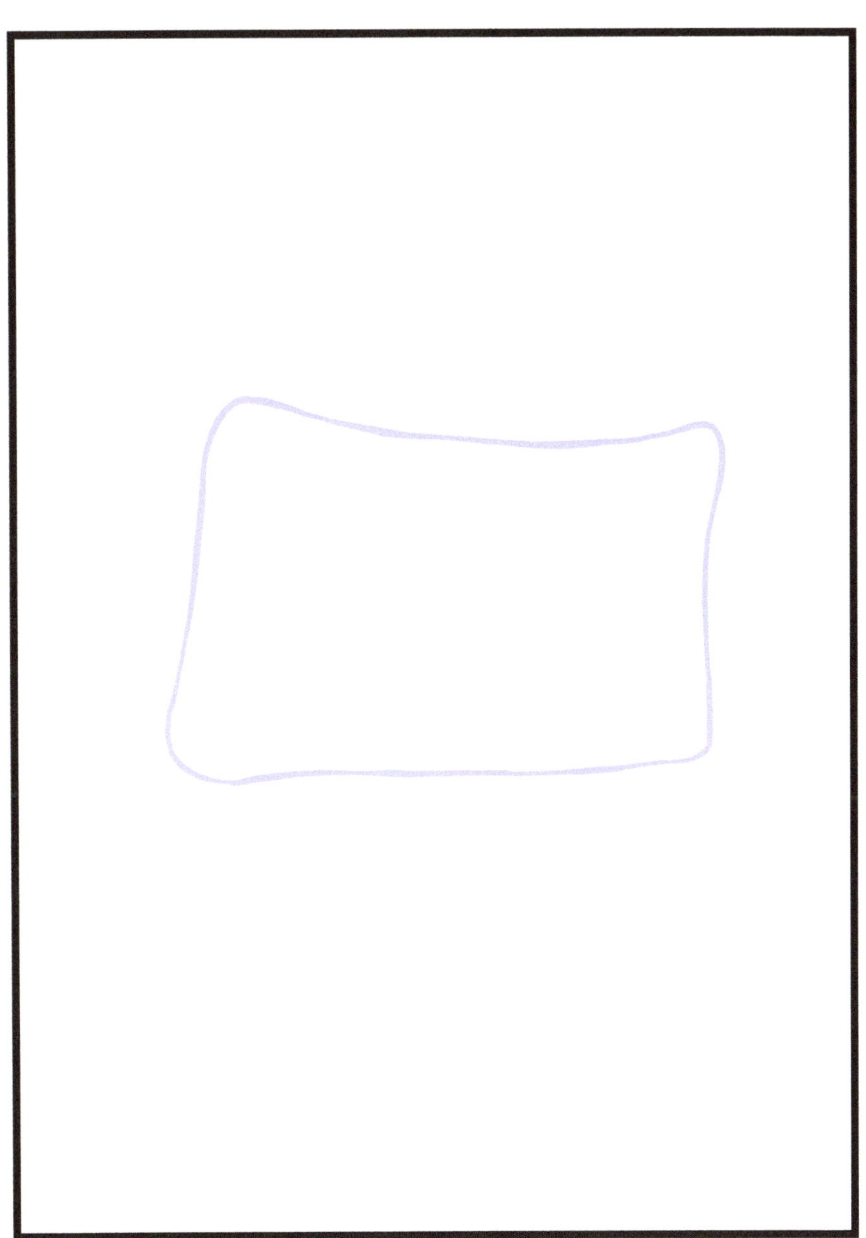

Calf

1. 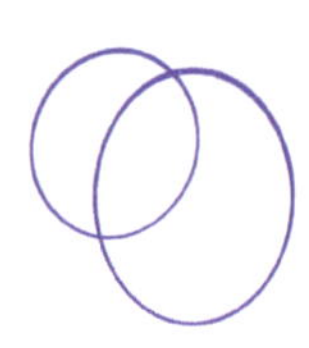

2. 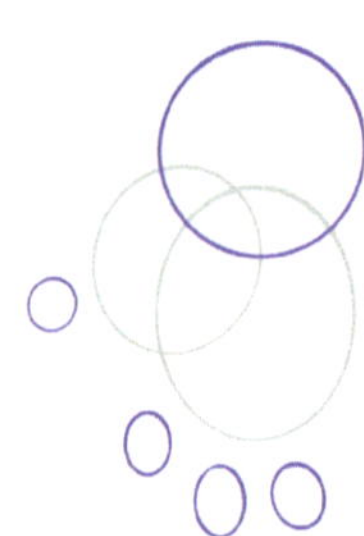

3. 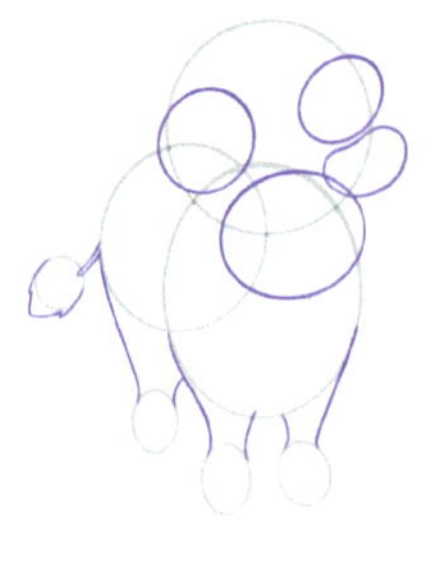

4. 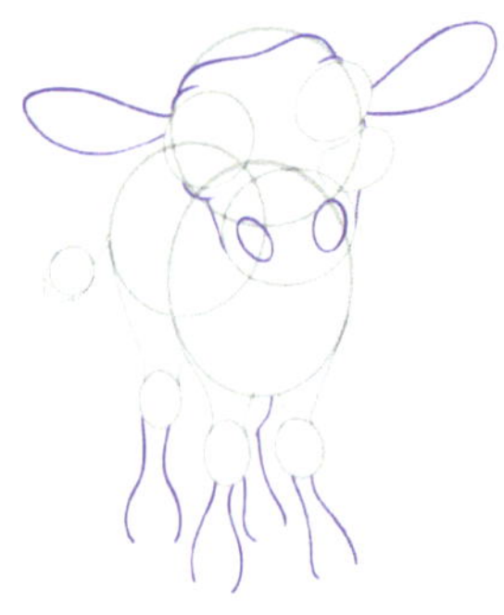

5. 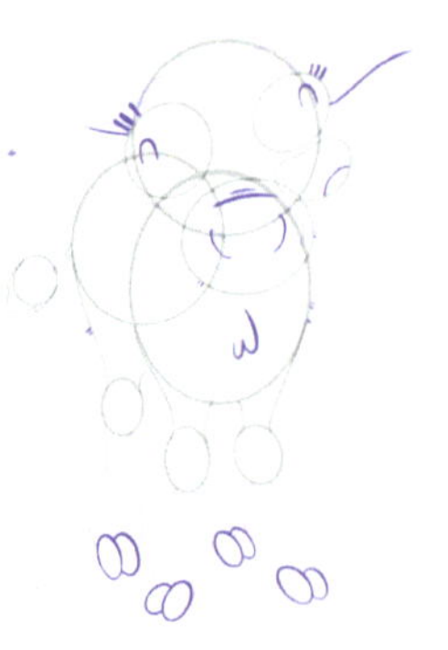

6. 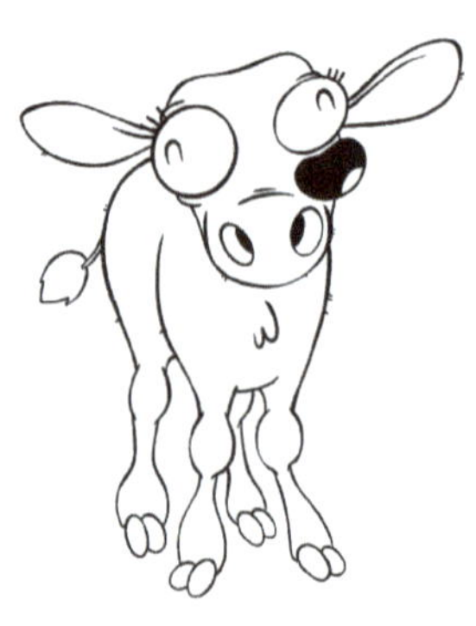

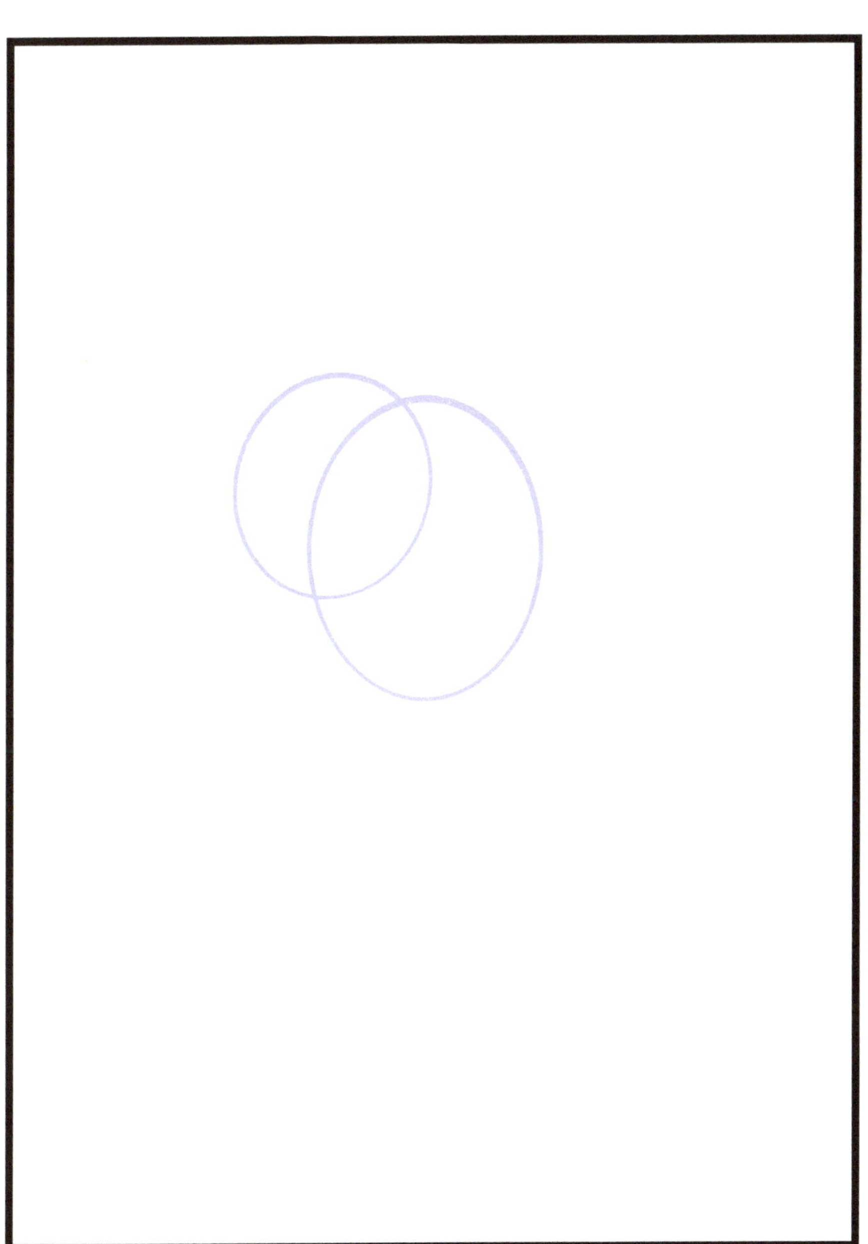

Goat

1.

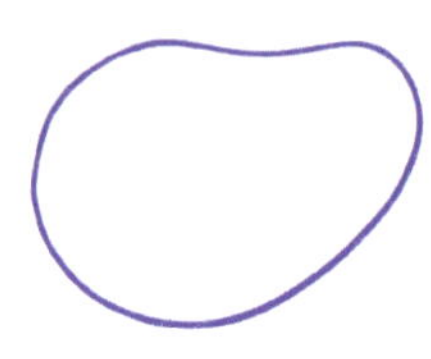

2.

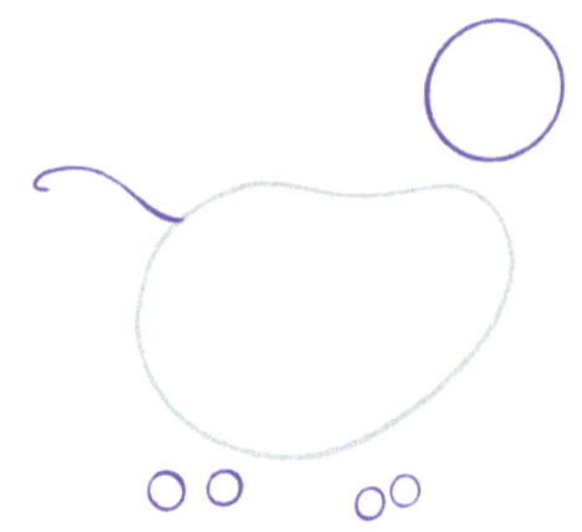

3.

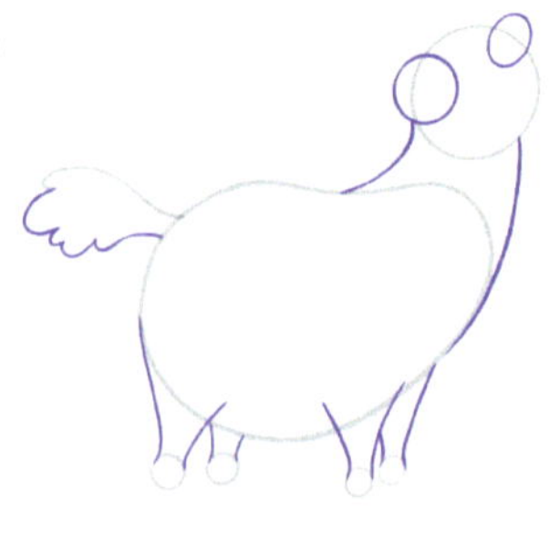

4.

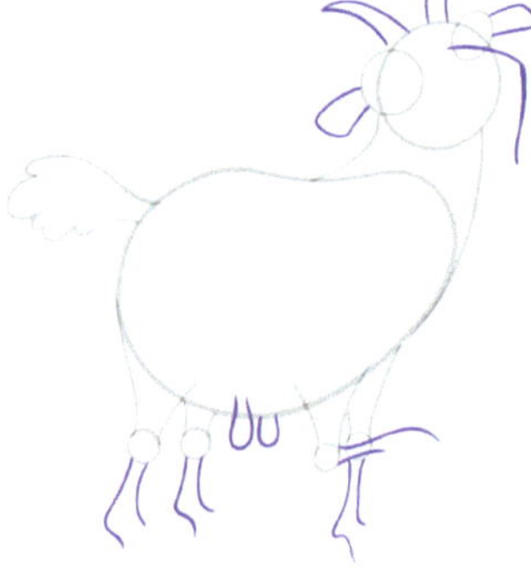

5.

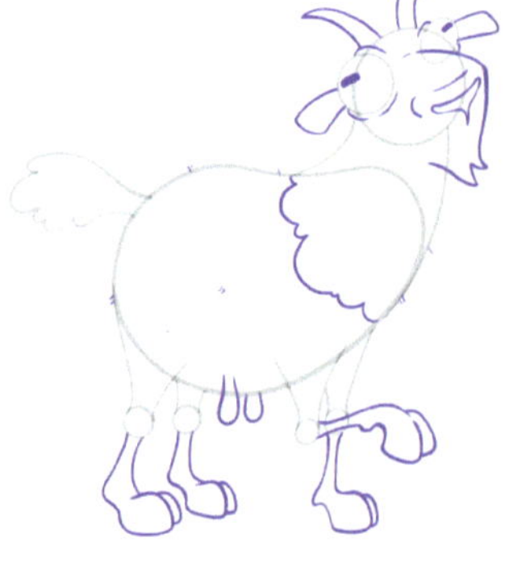

6.

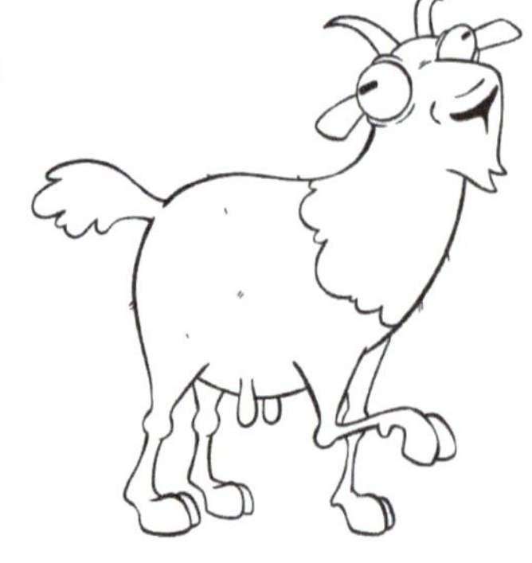

Goat

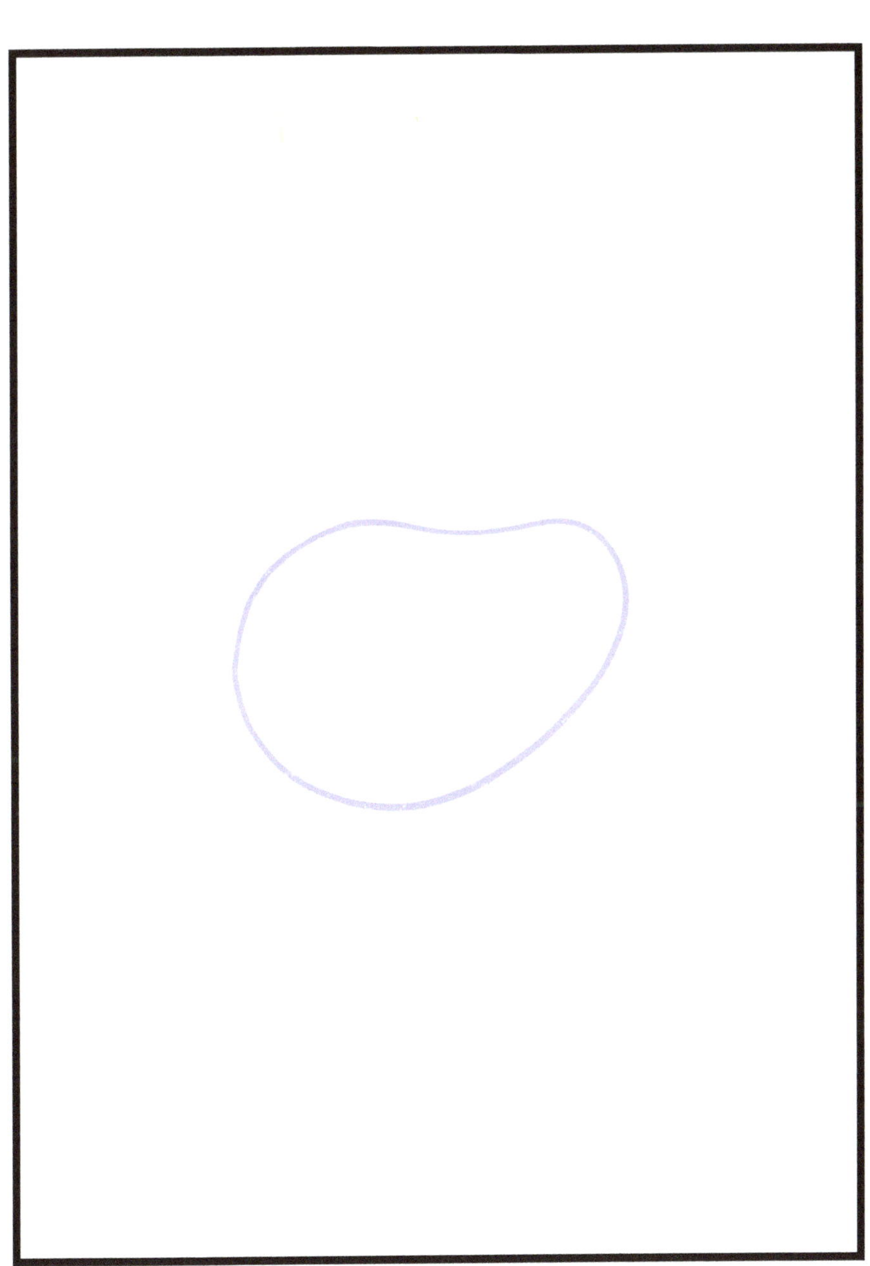

Duck

1.

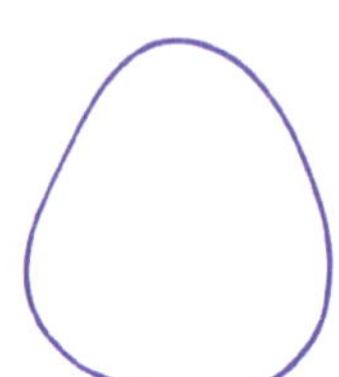

2.

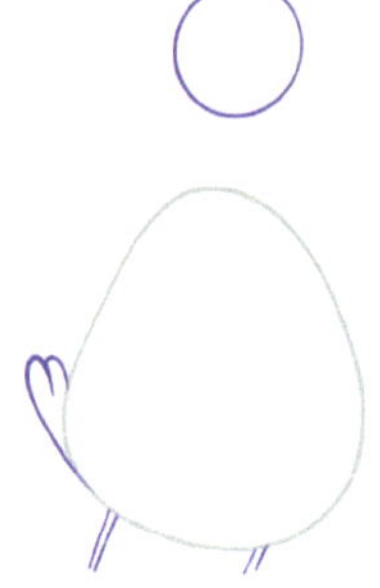

3.

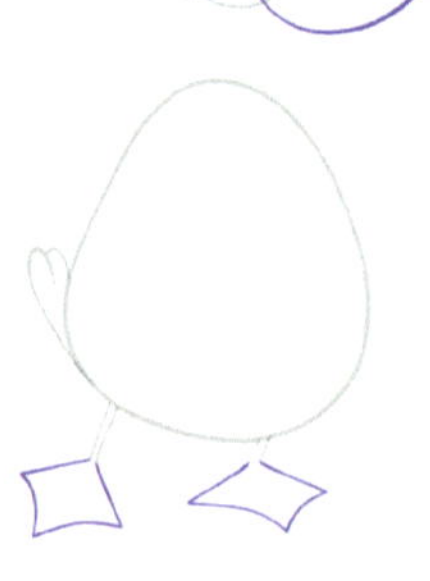

4.

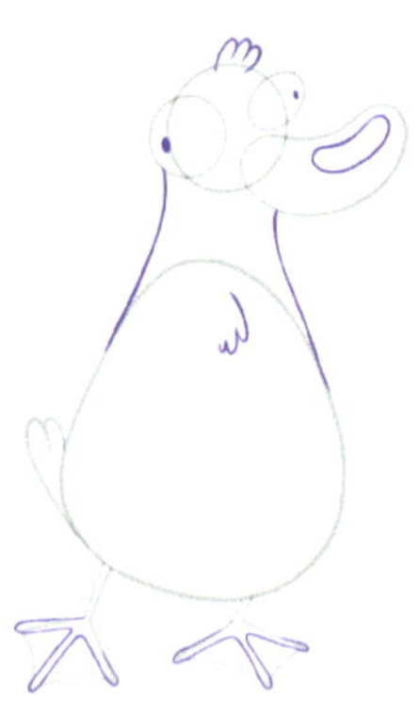

5.

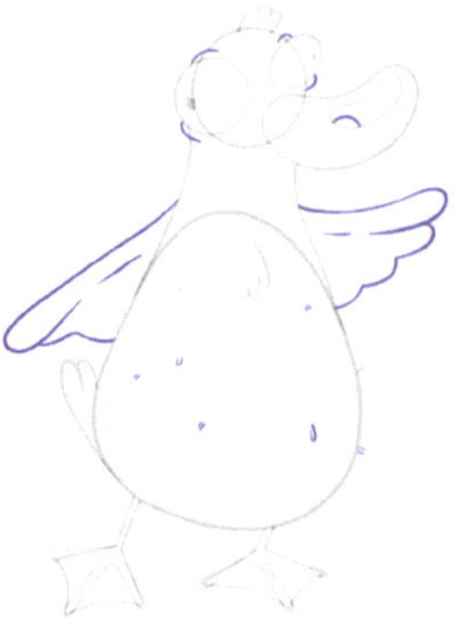

6.

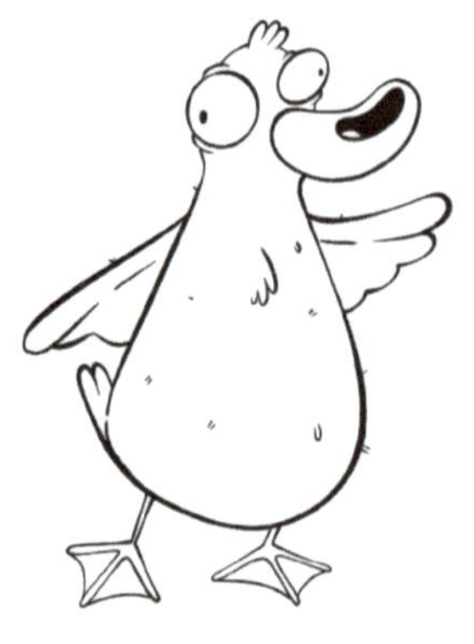

Duck

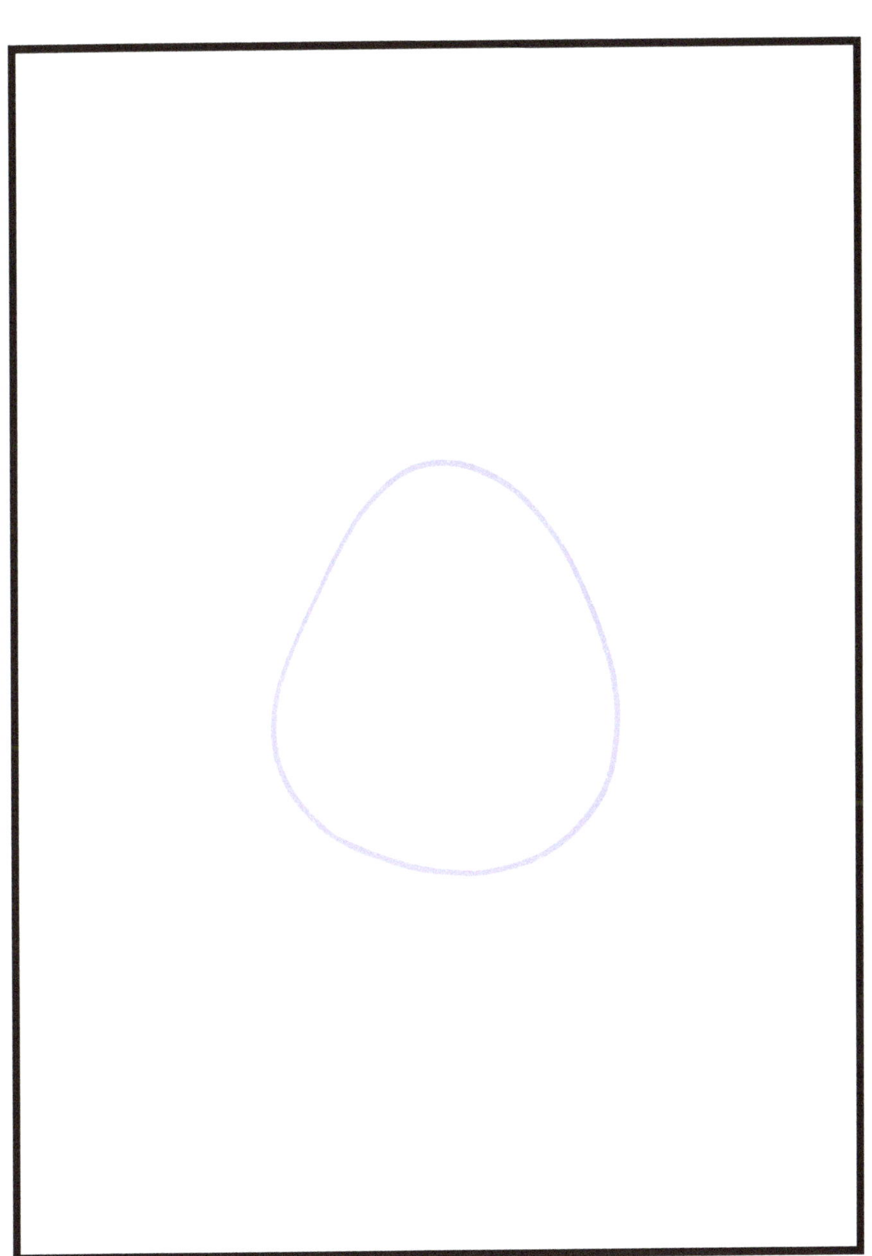

Rabbit

1. 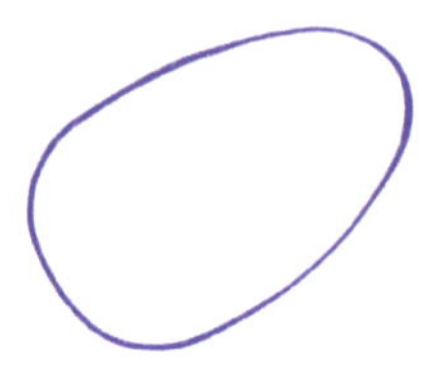

2. 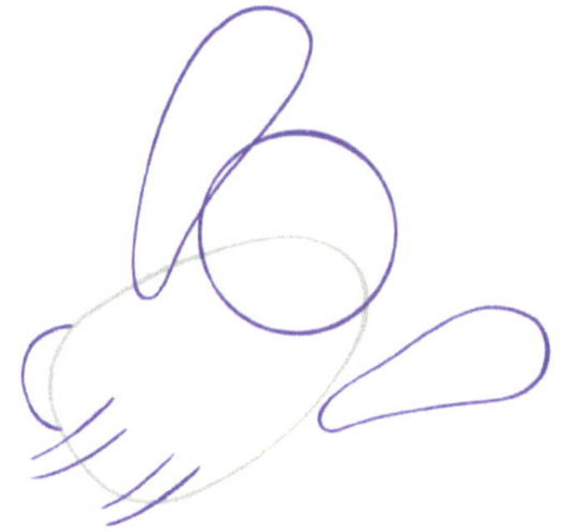

3. 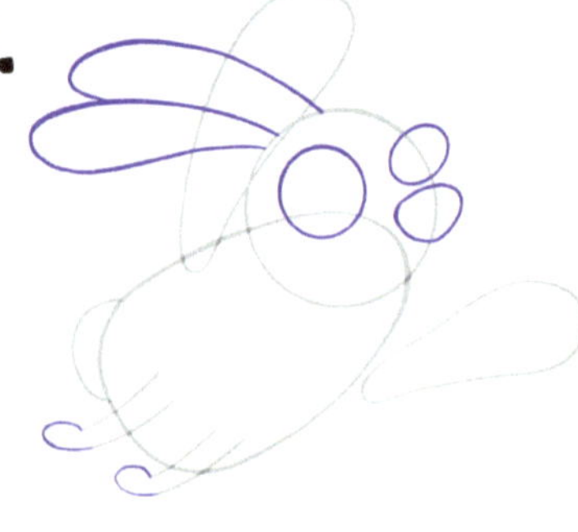

4. 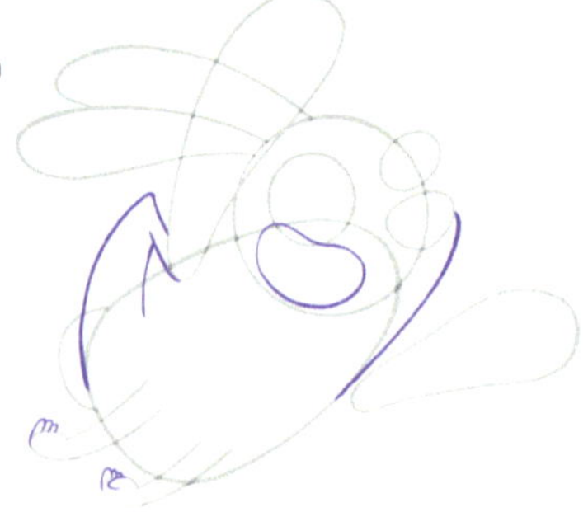

5. 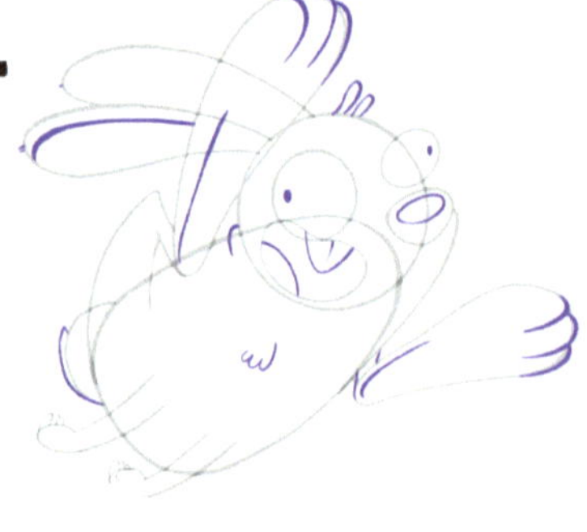

6. 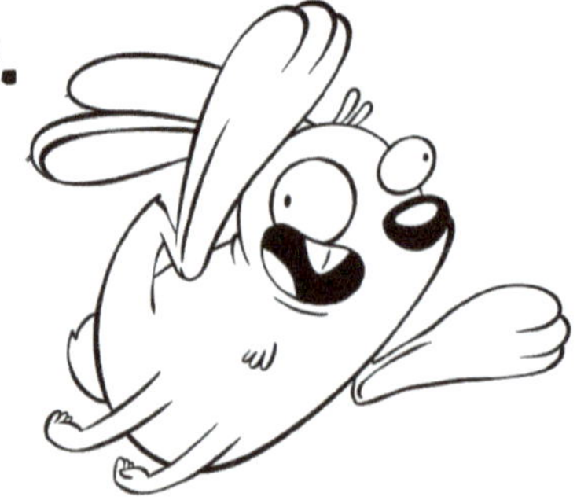

Rabbit

Goose

1.

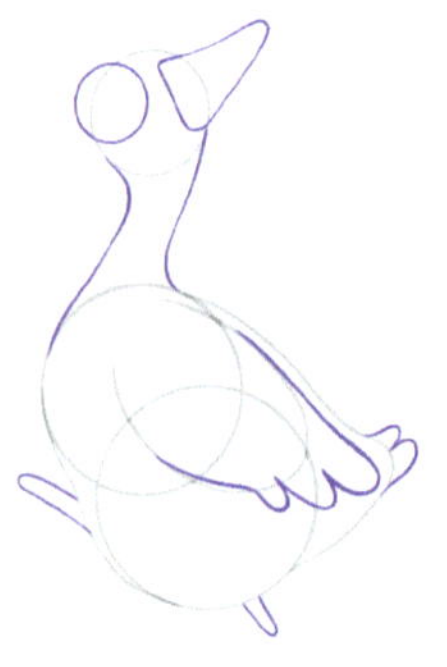

2.

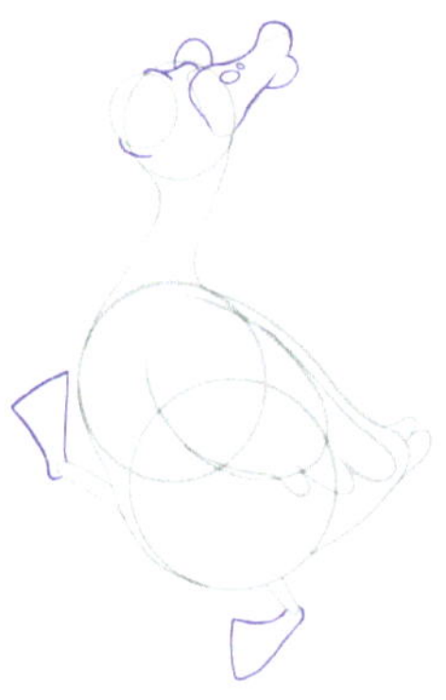

3.

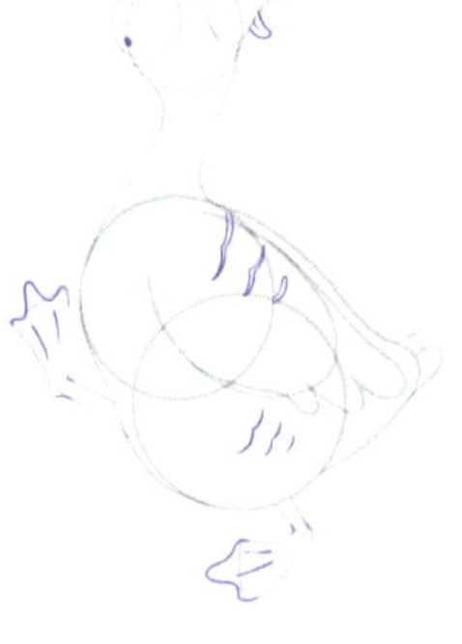

4.

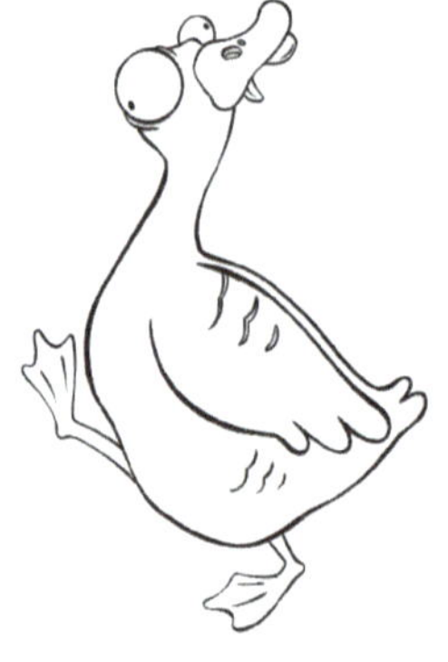

5.

6.

Goose

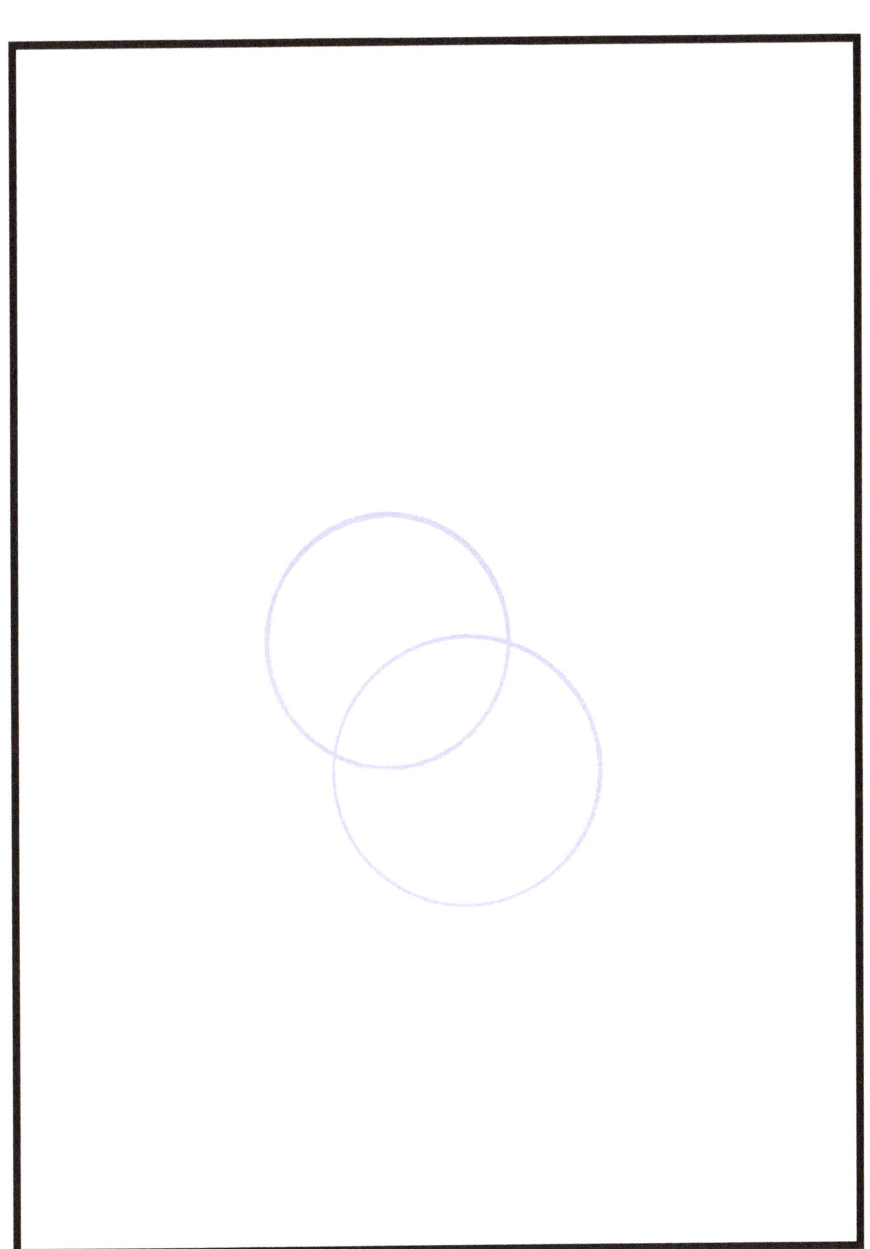

Barn Cat

1.
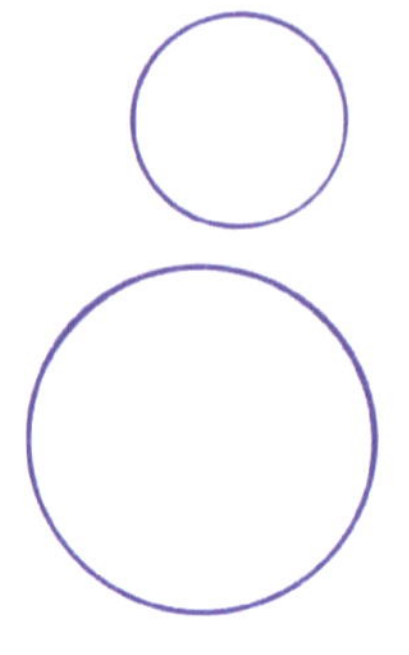

2.
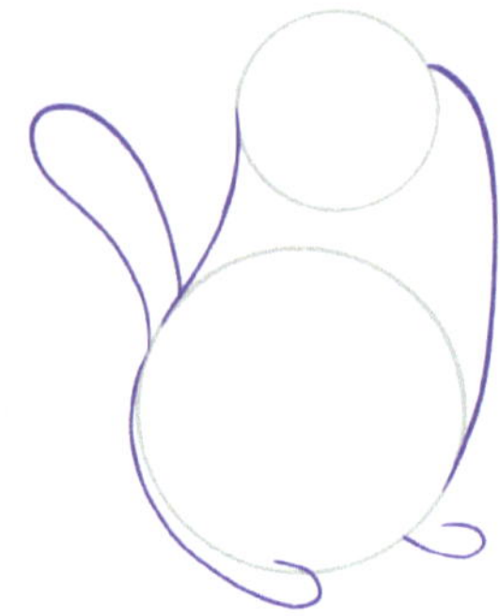

3.
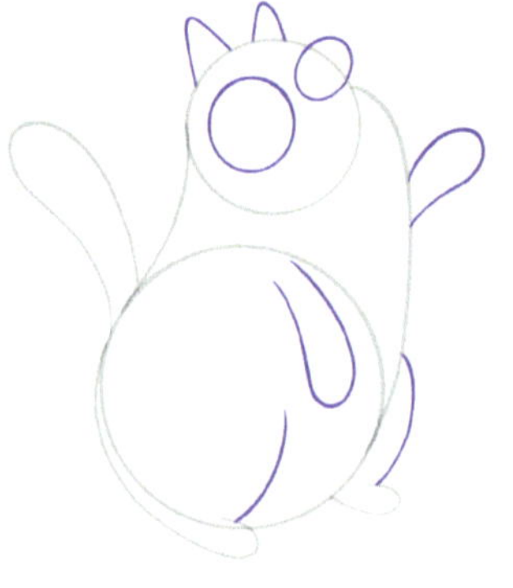

4.
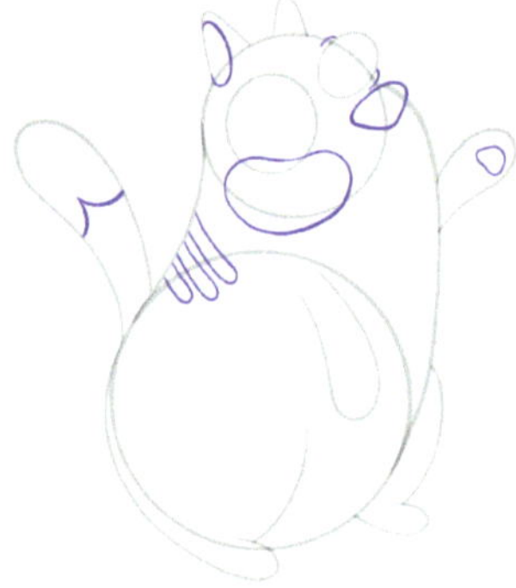

5.
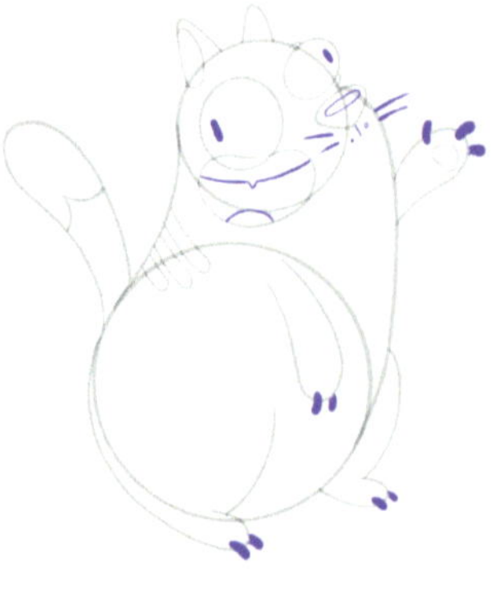

6.
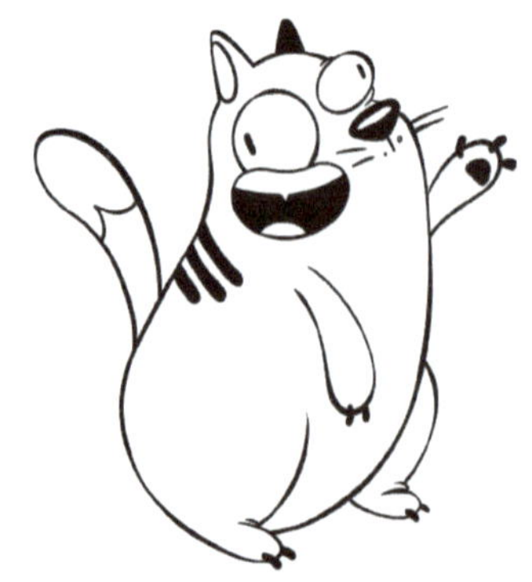

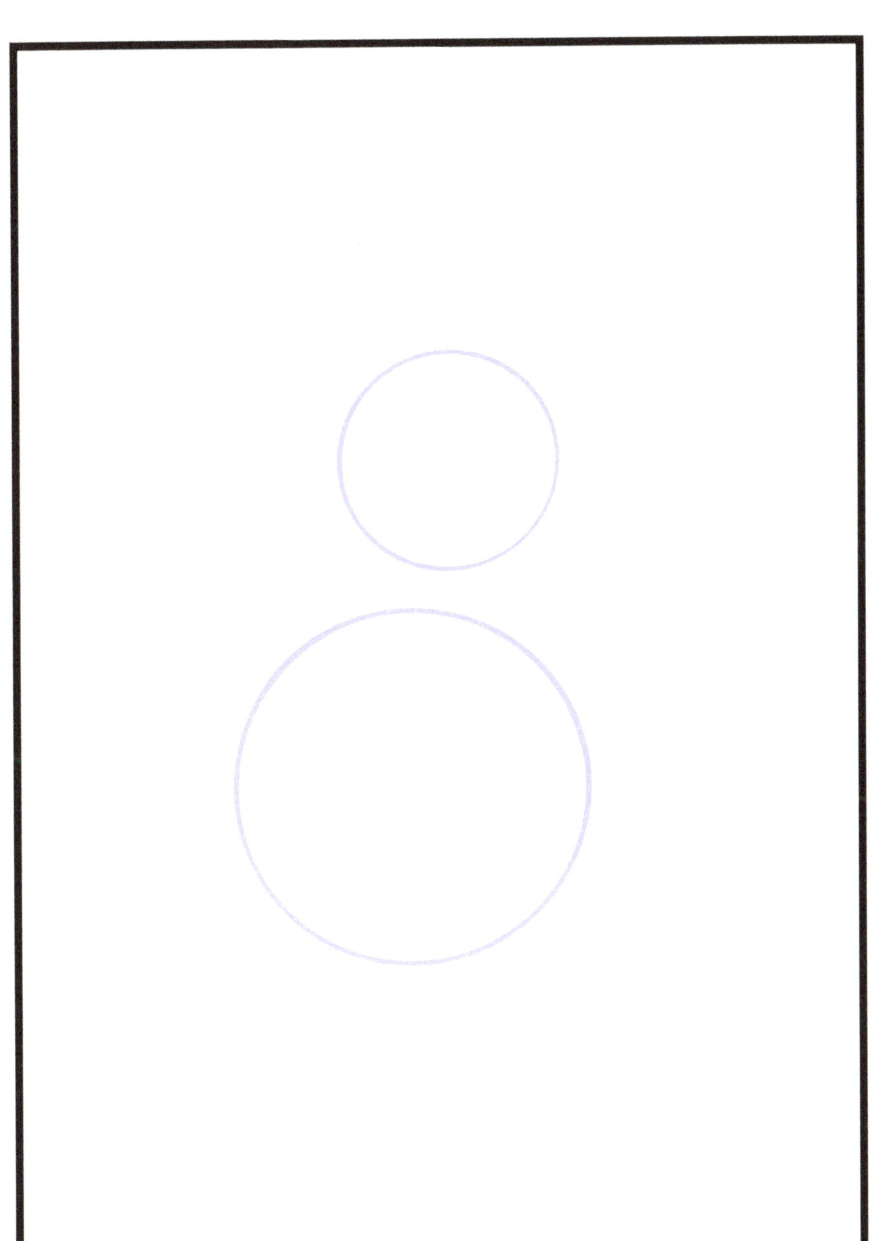

Border Collie

1.

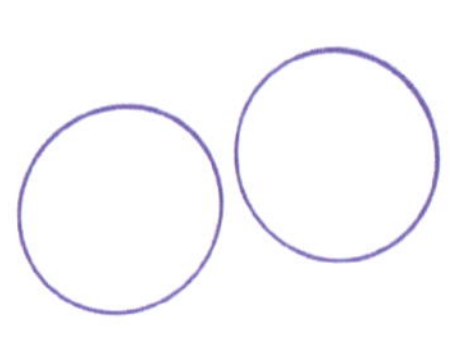

2.

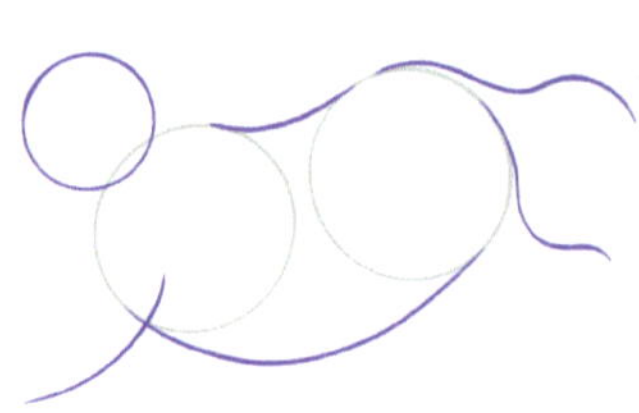

3.

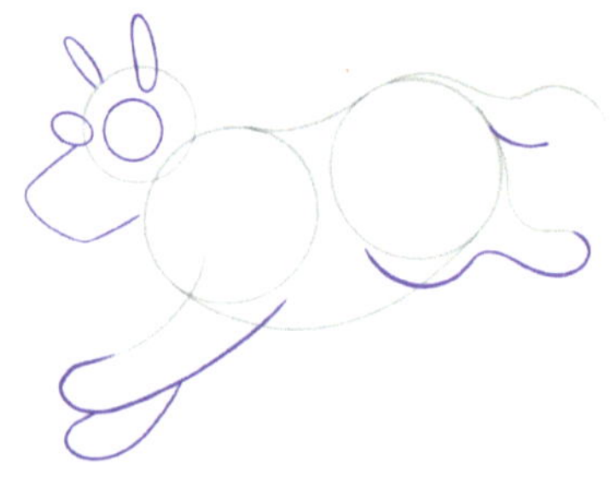

4.

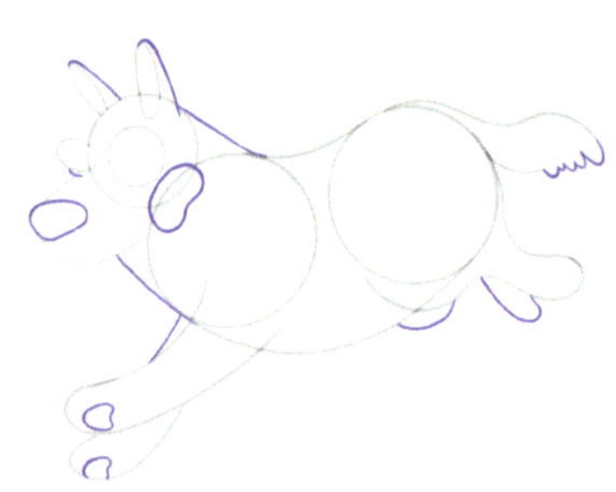

5.

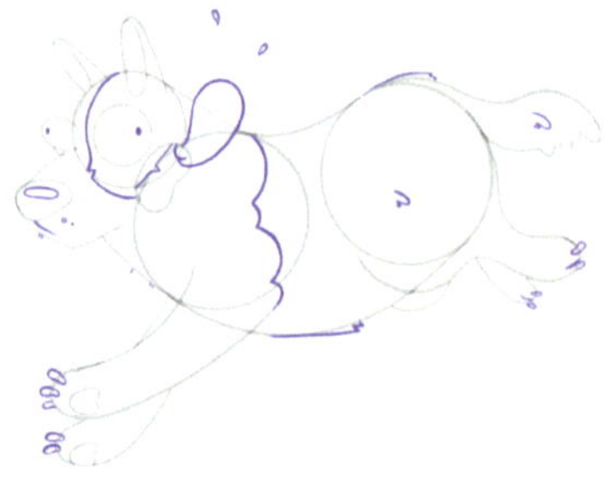

6.

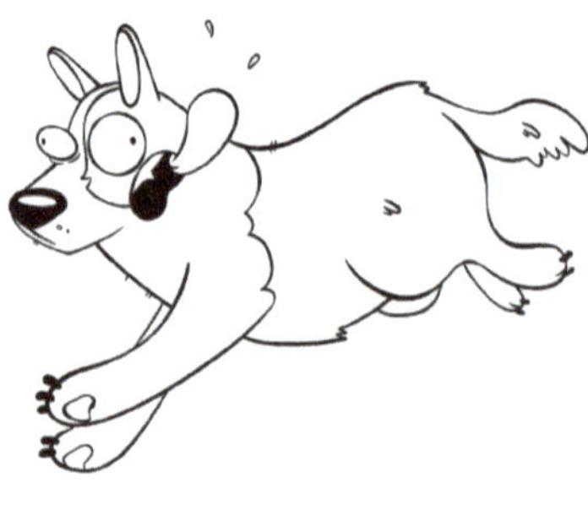

Border Collie

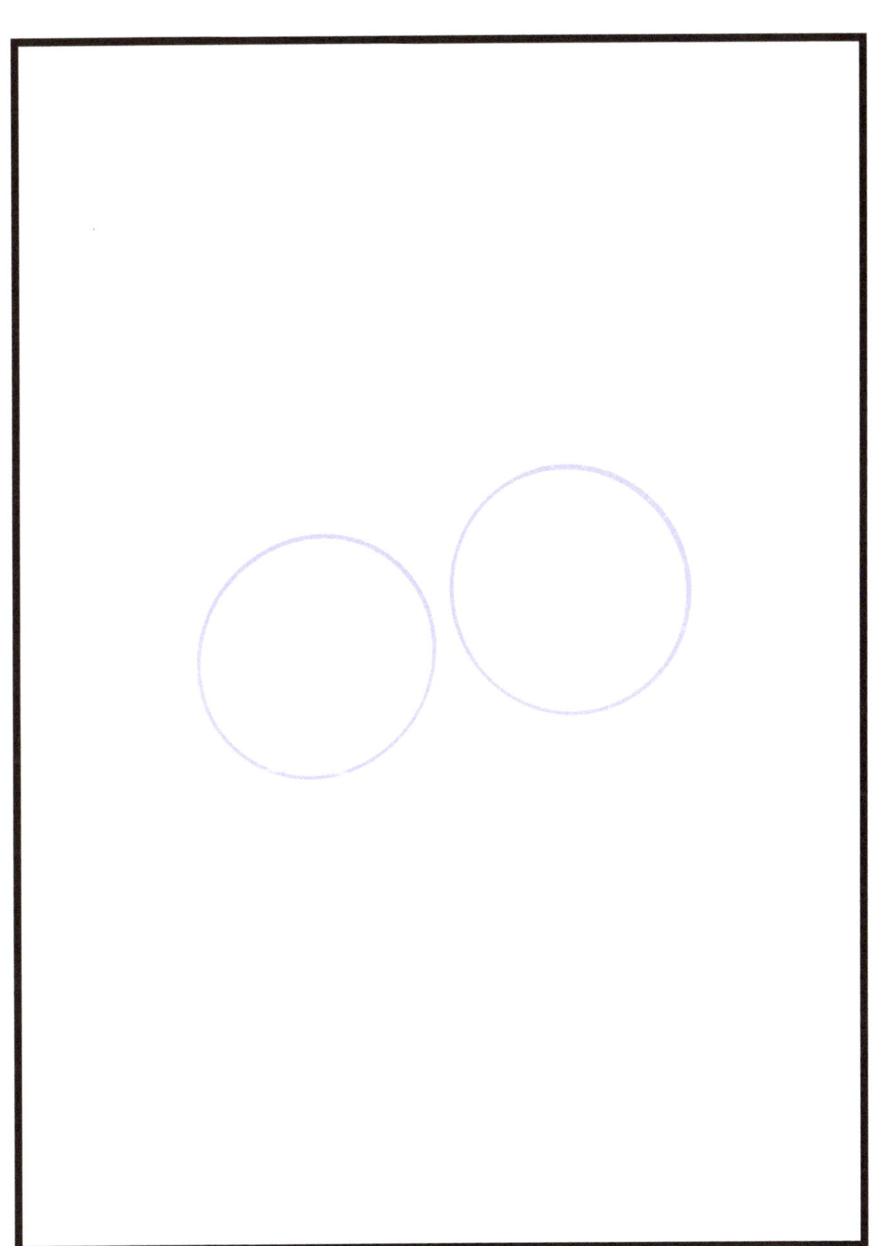

Field Mouse

1.

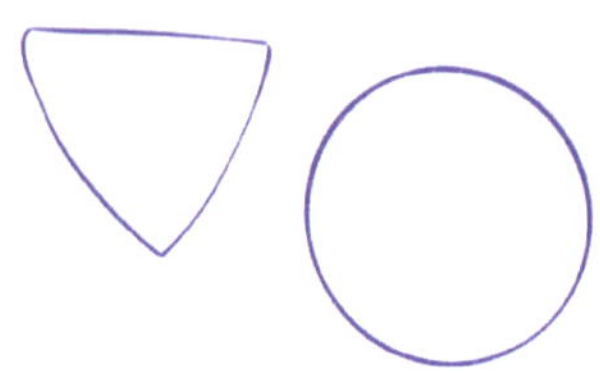

2.

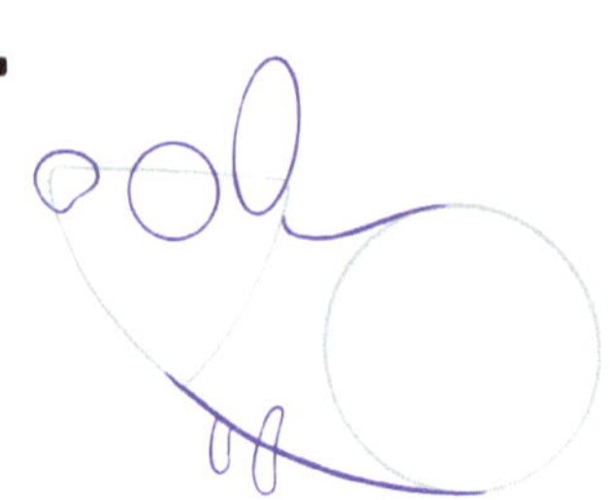

3.

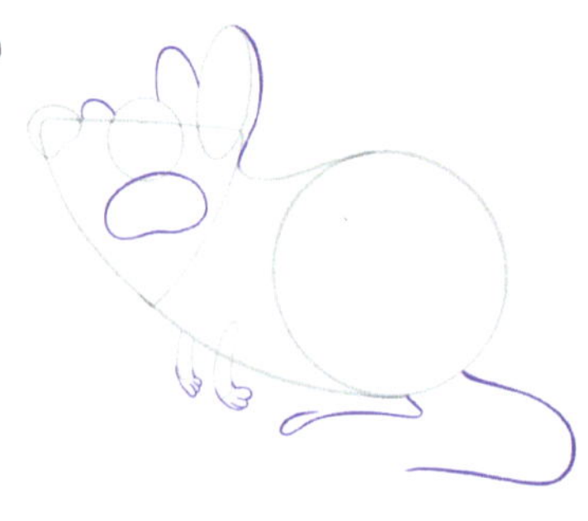

4.

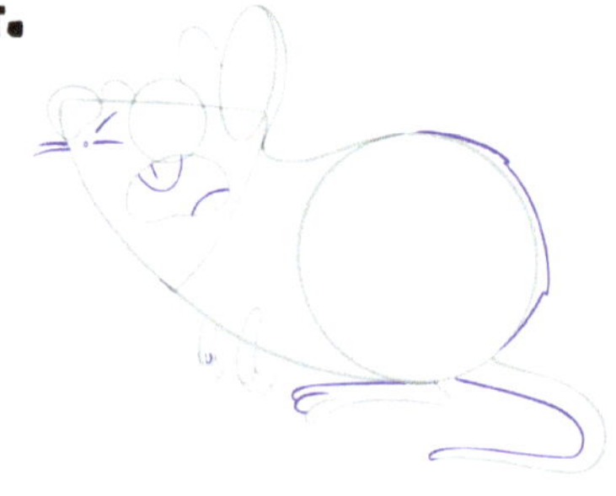

5.

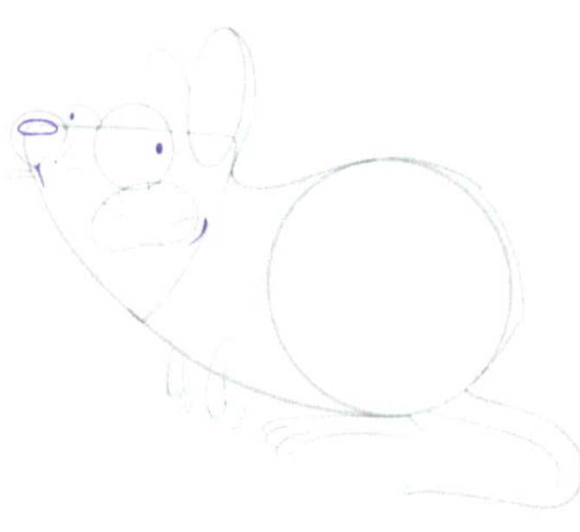

6.

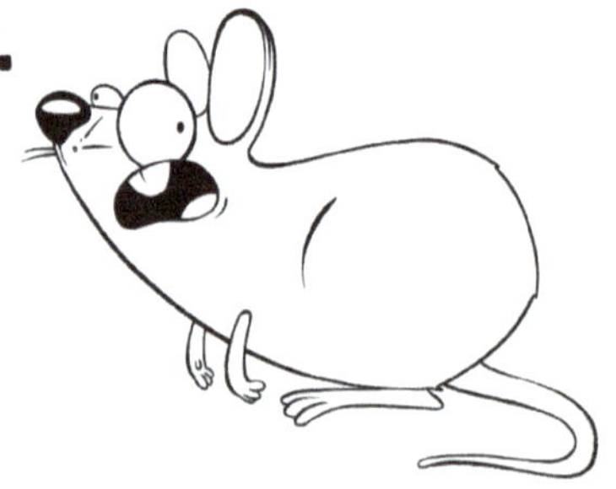

Field Mouse

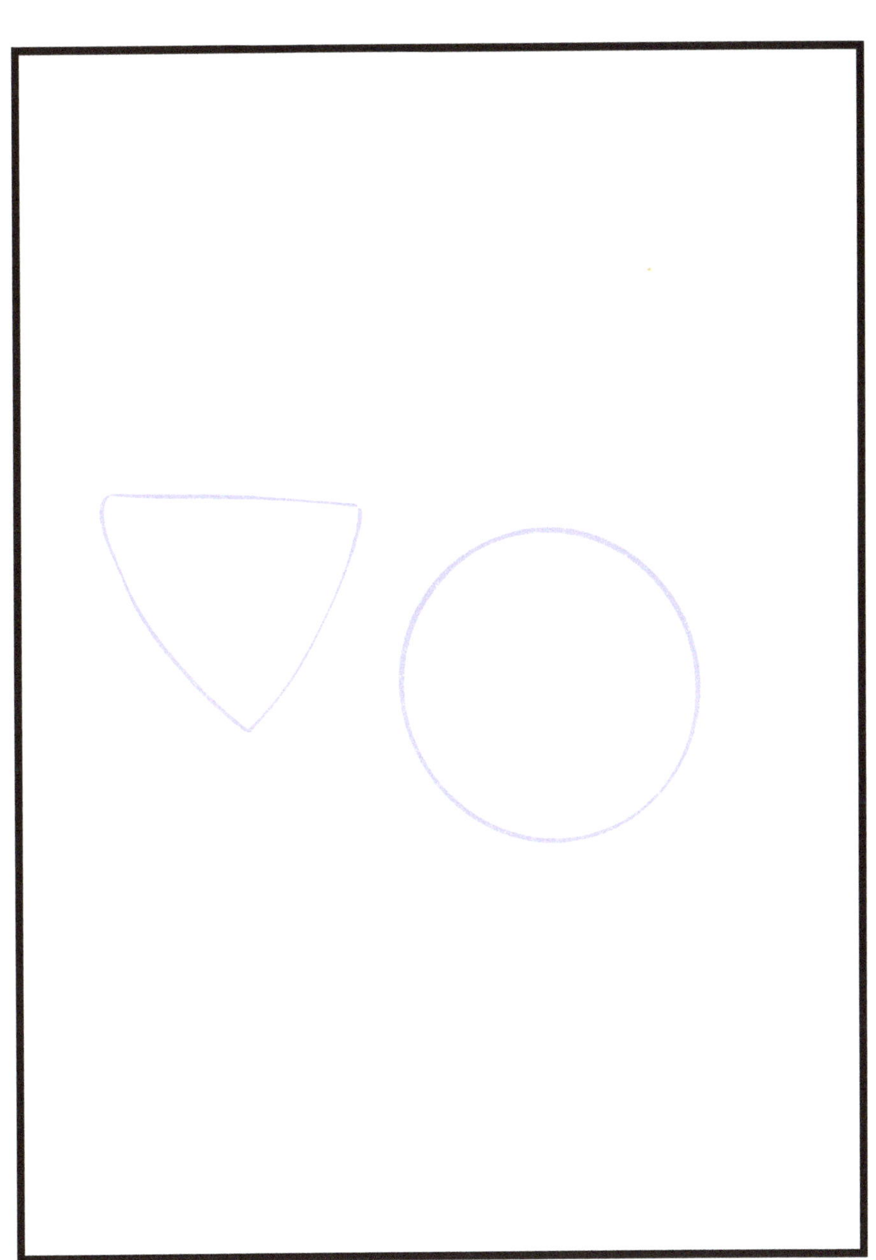

Donkey

1.

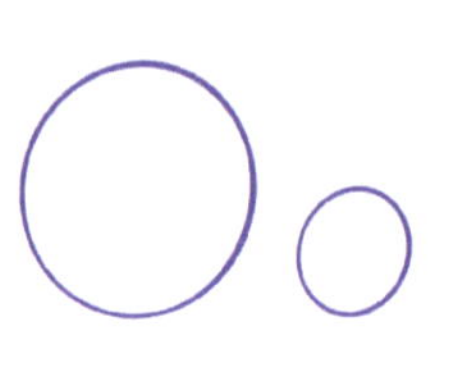

2.

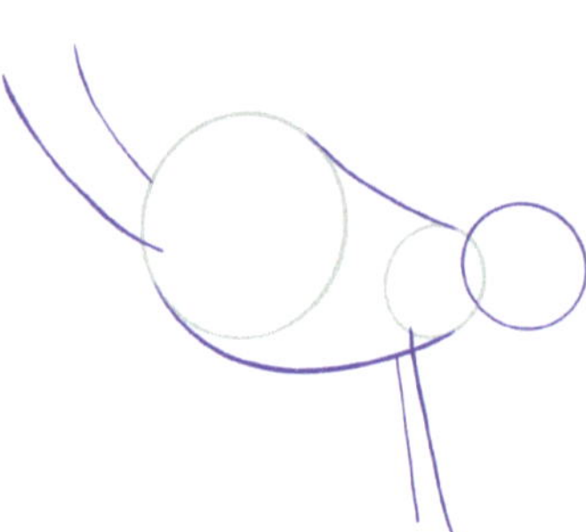

3.

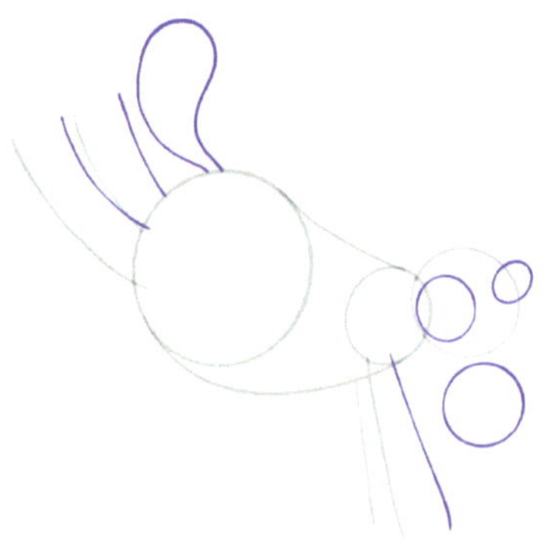

4.

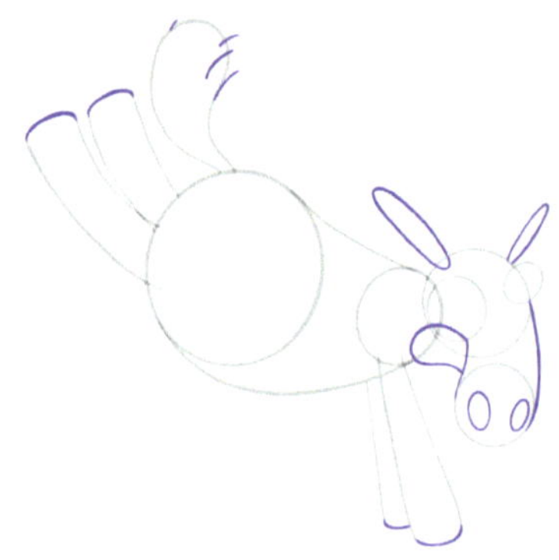

5.

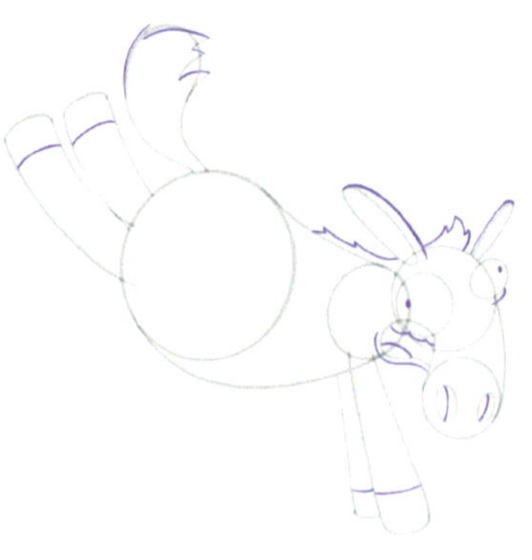

6.

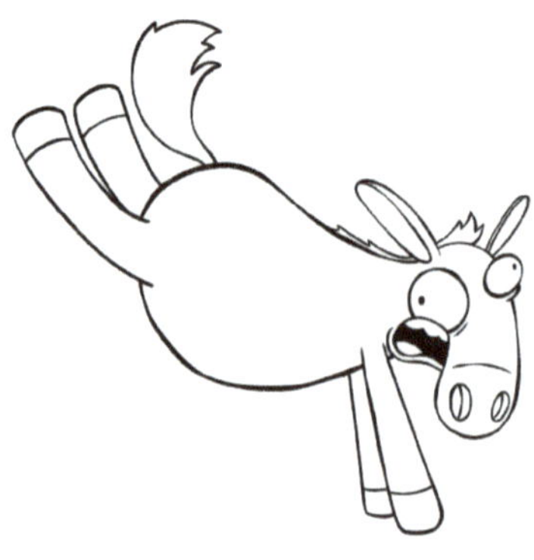

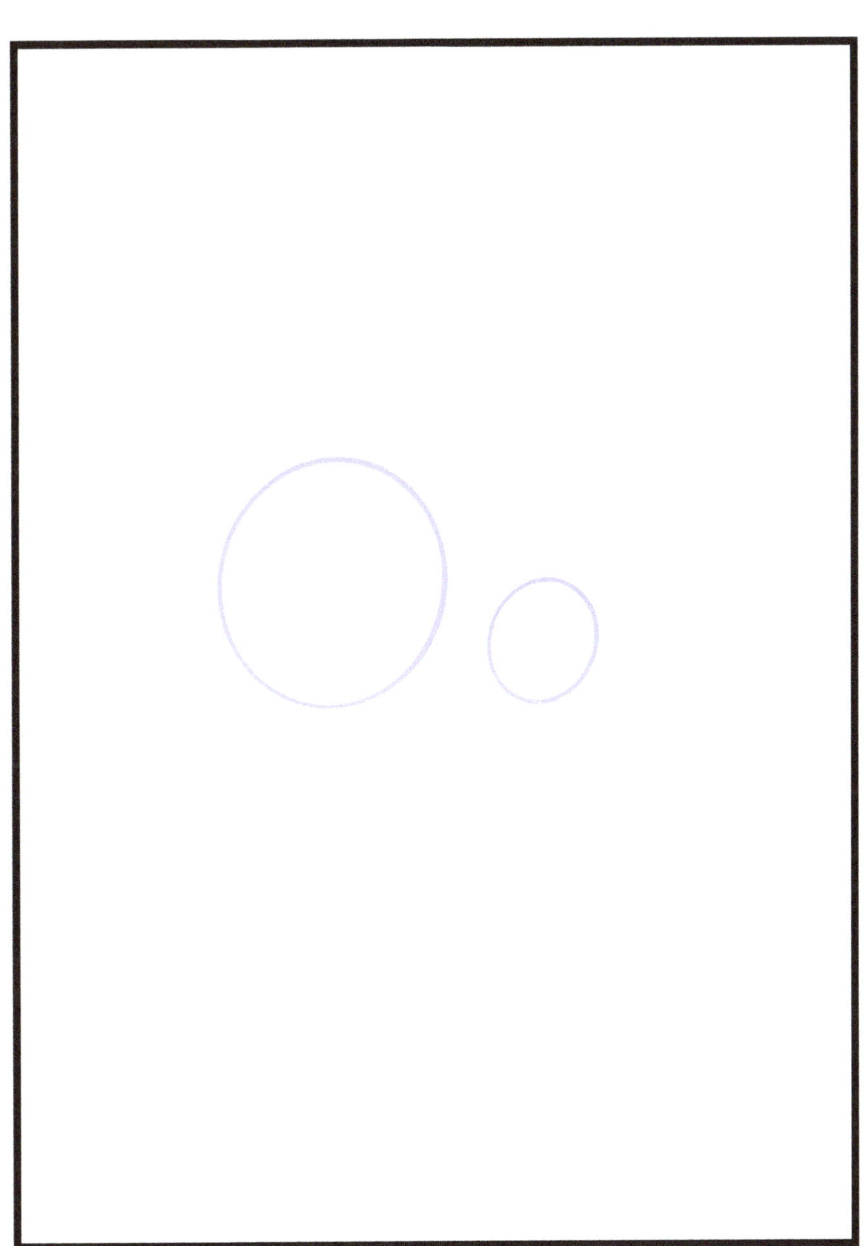

Horse

1.

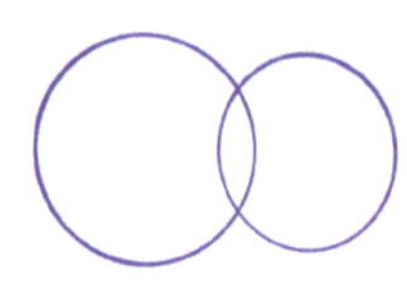

2.

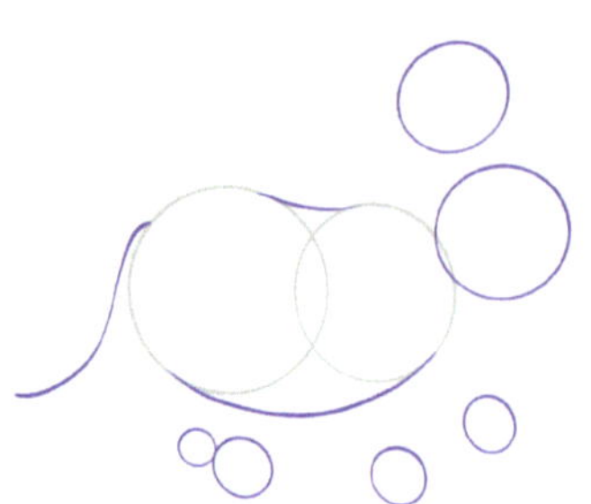

3.

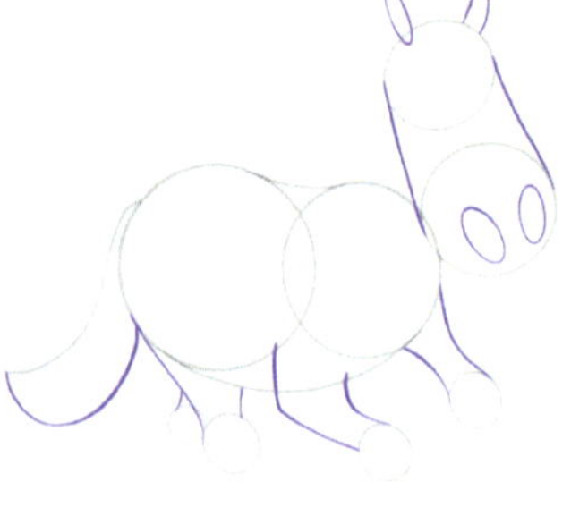

4.

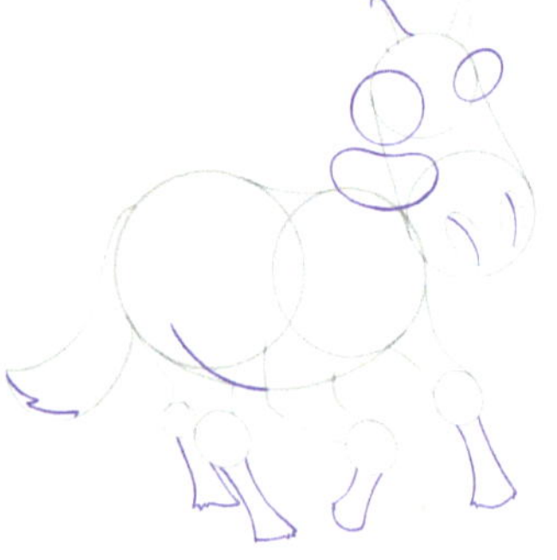

5.

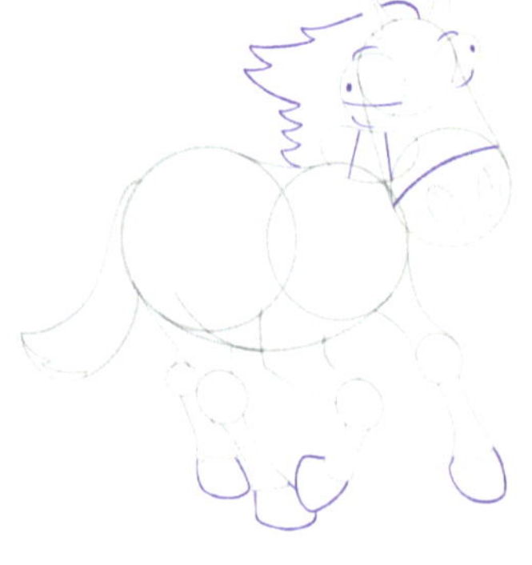

6.

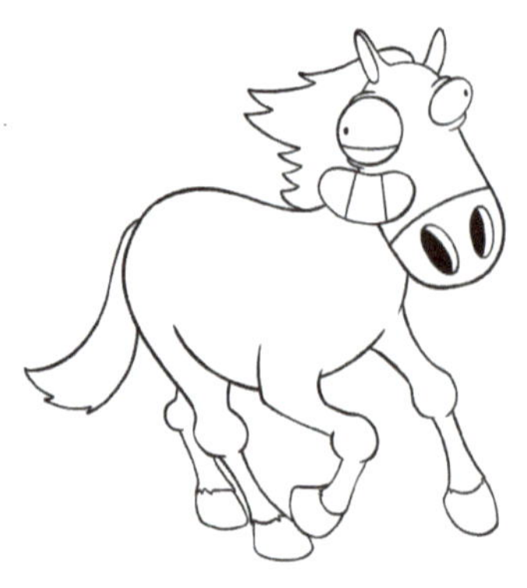

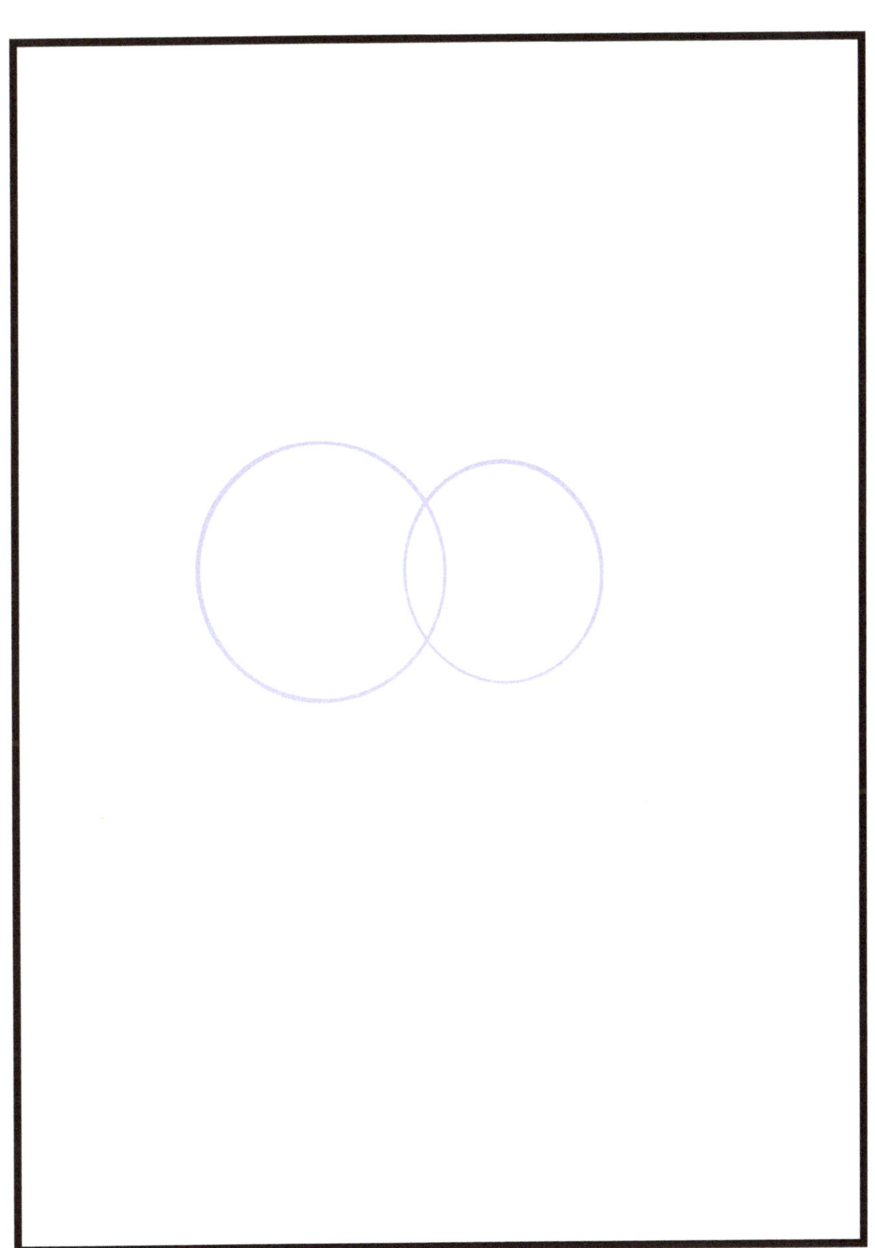

Colt

1. 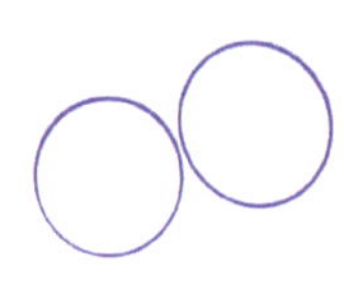

2. 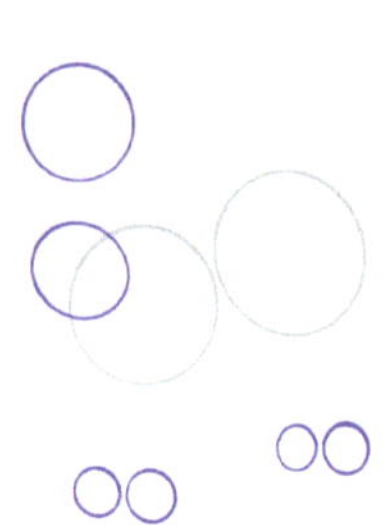

3. 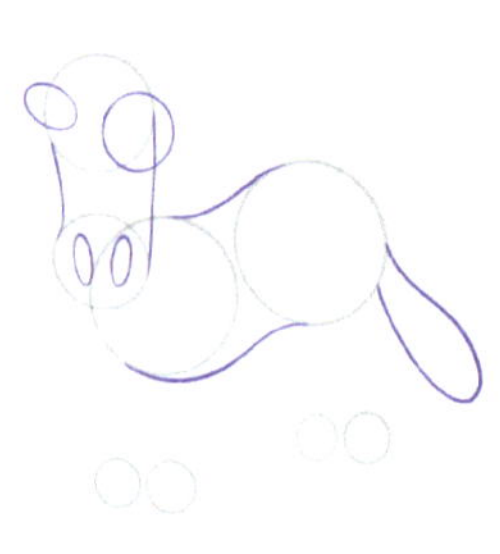

4. 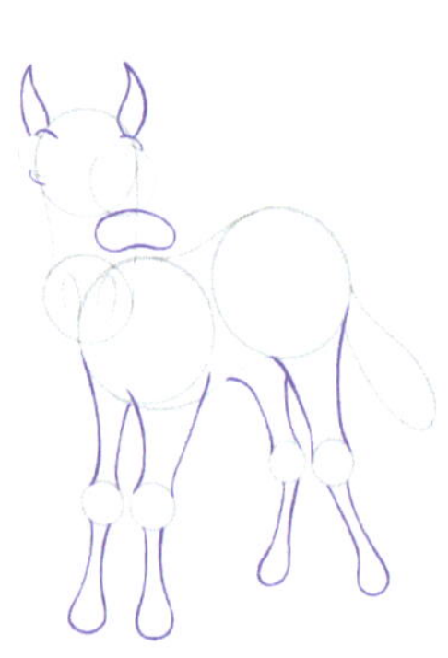

5. 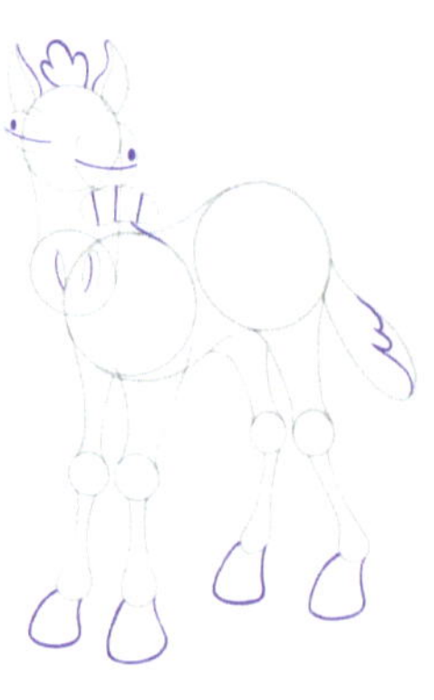

6. 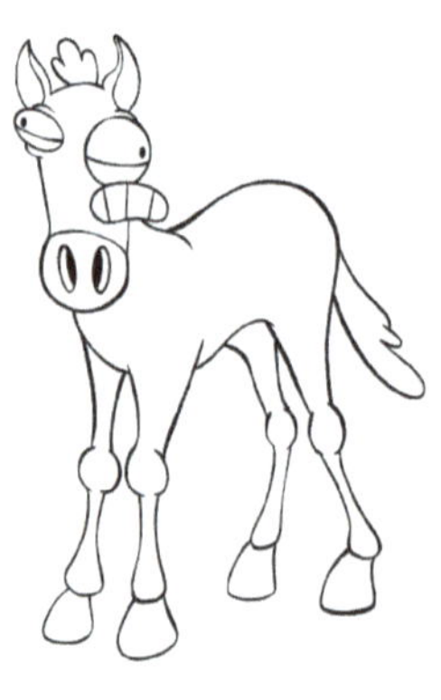

Colt

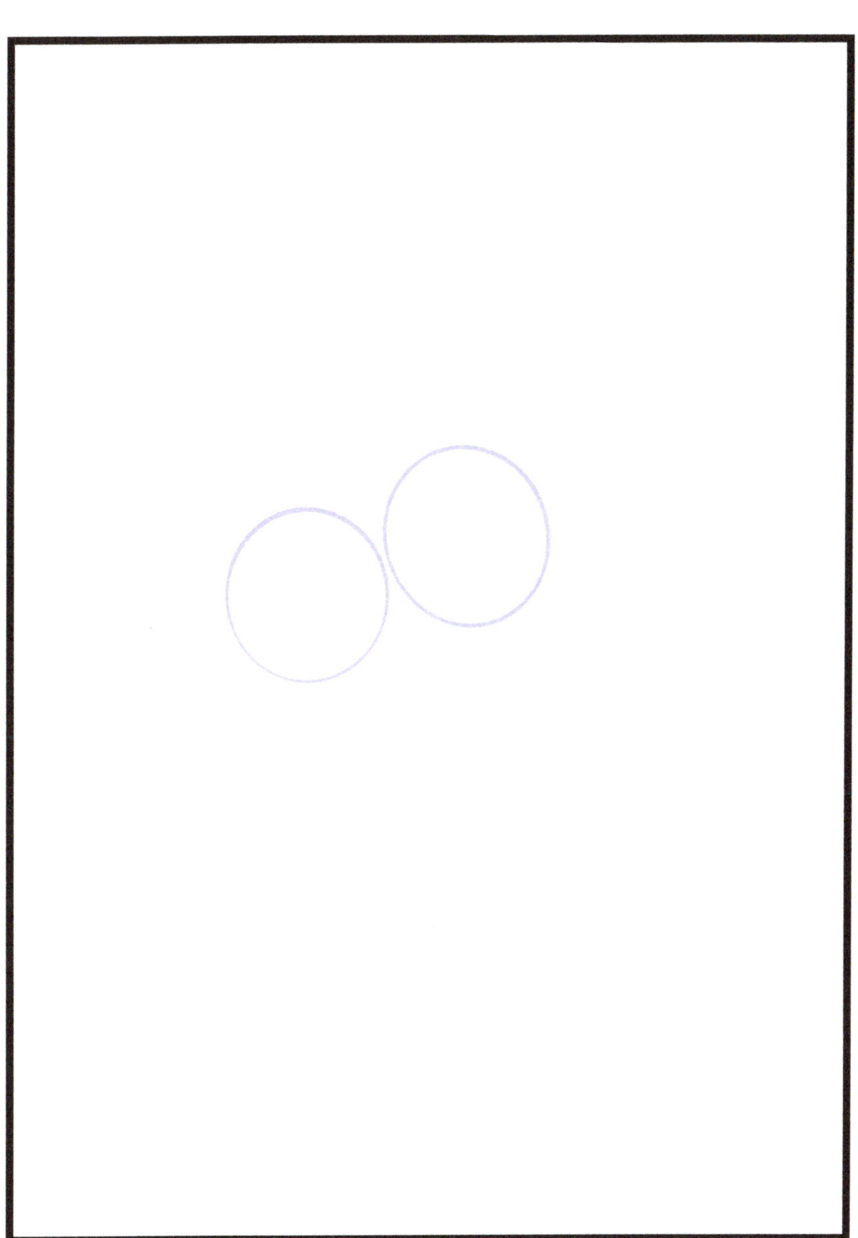

Llama

1.

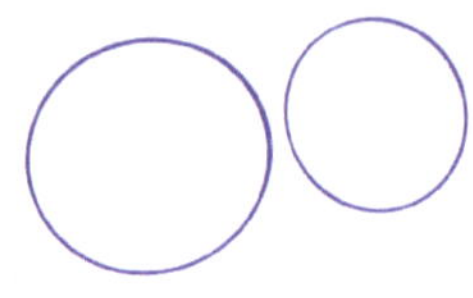

2.

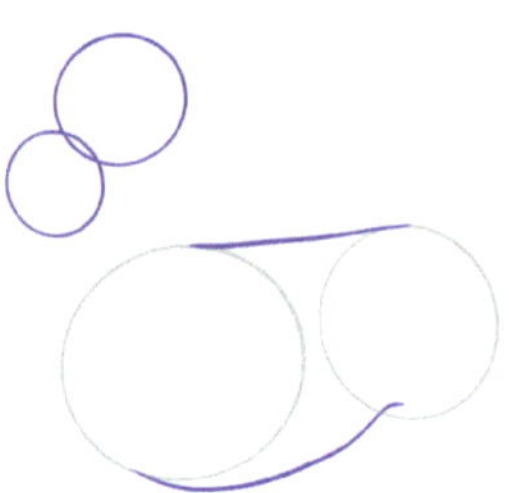

3.

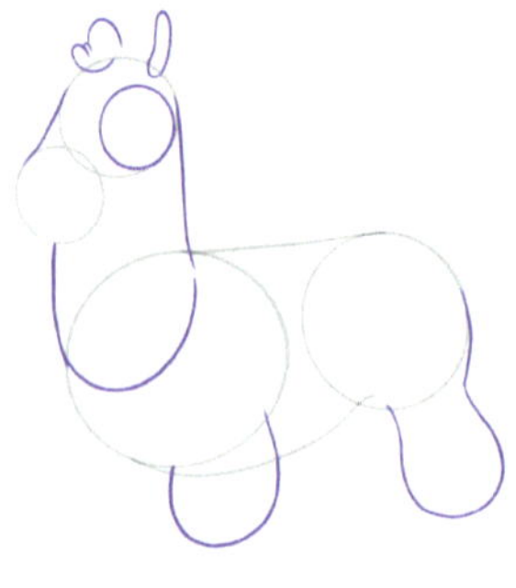

4.

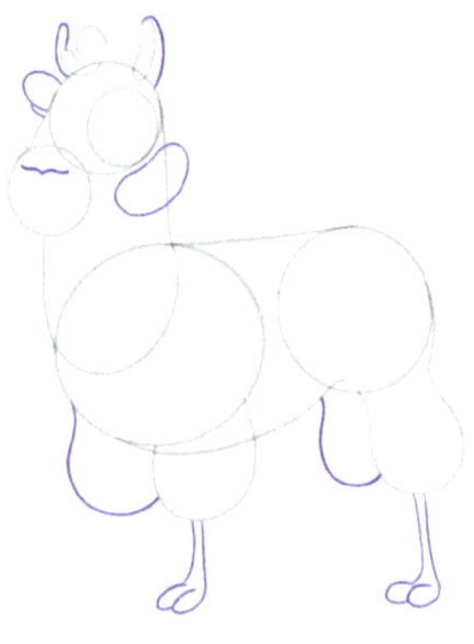

5.

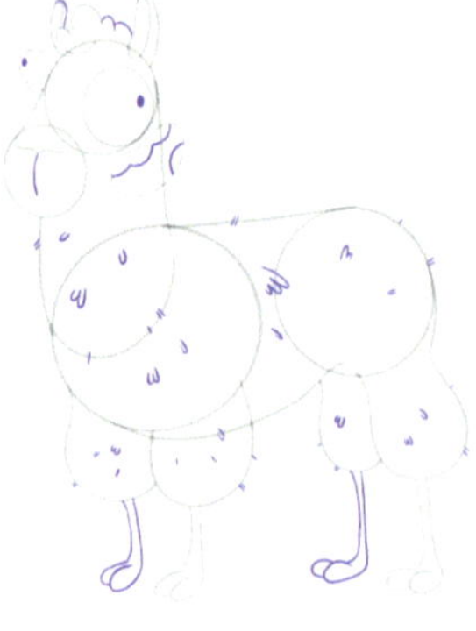

6.

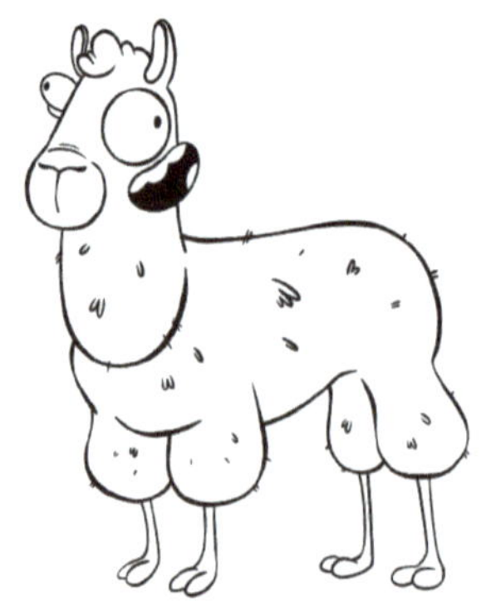

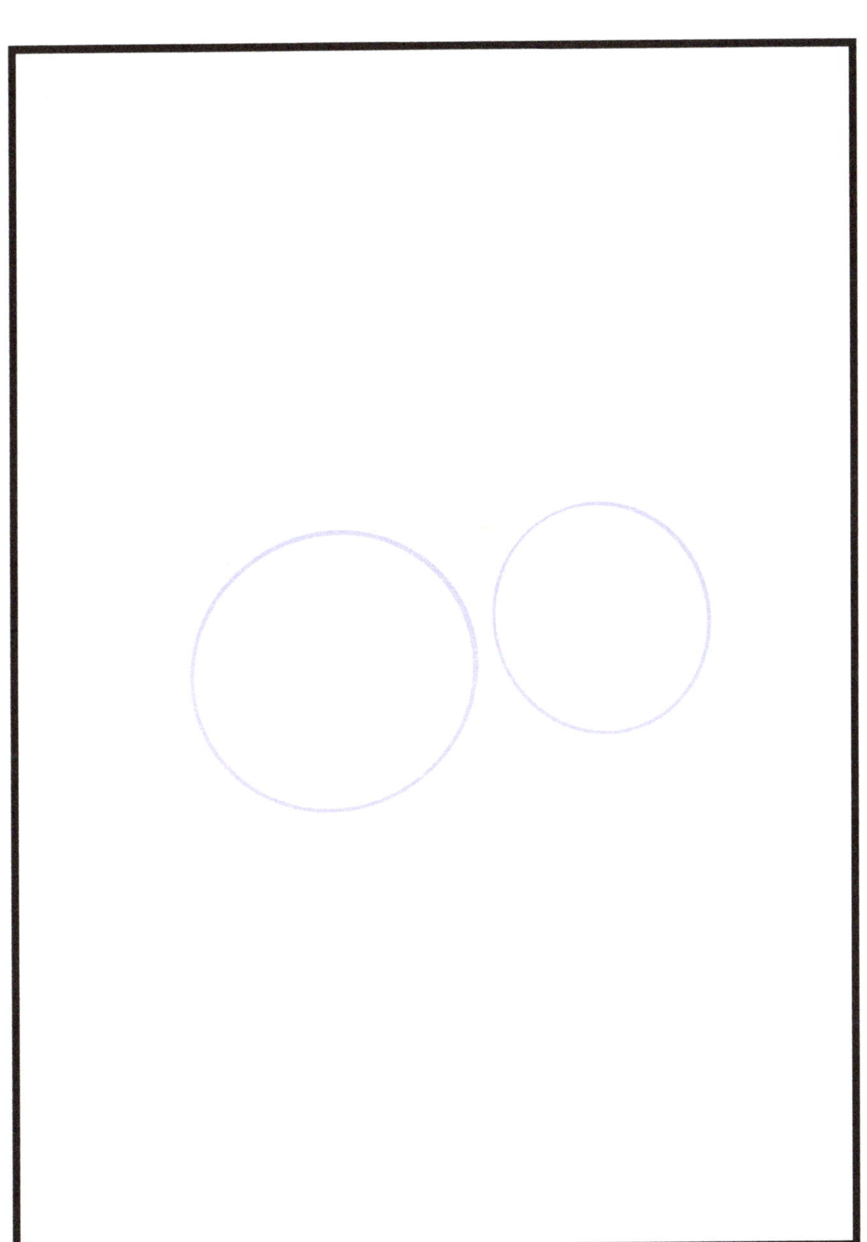

Honeybee

1.

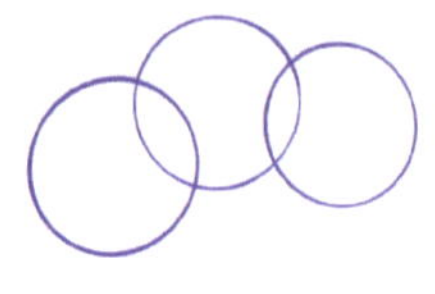

2.

3.

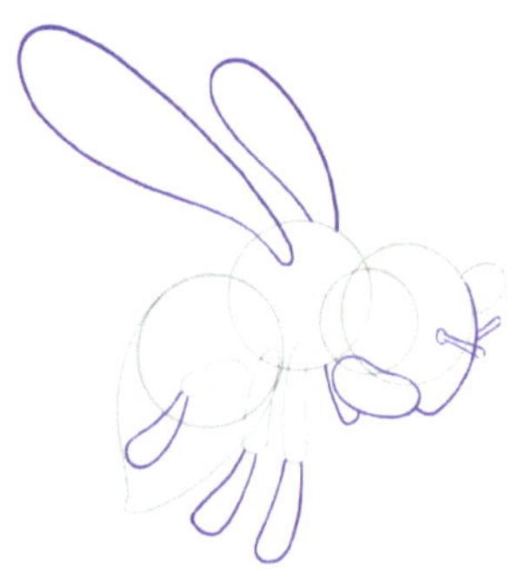

4.

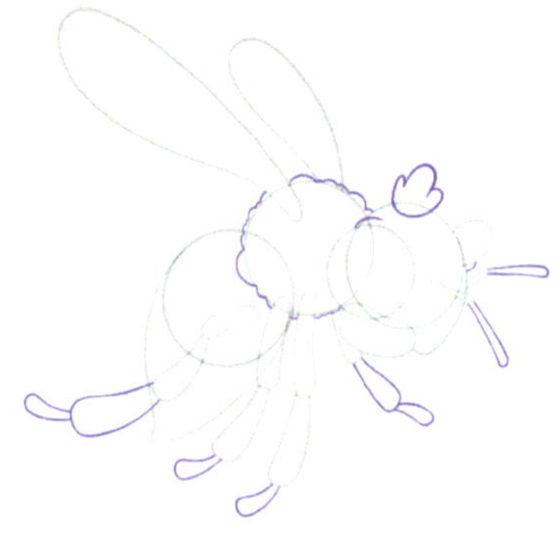

5.

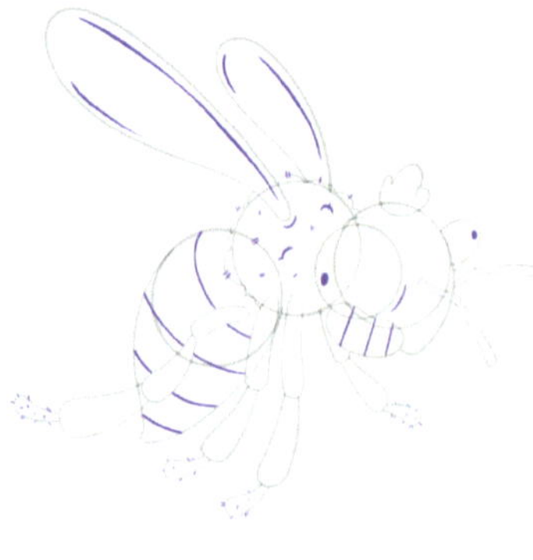

6.

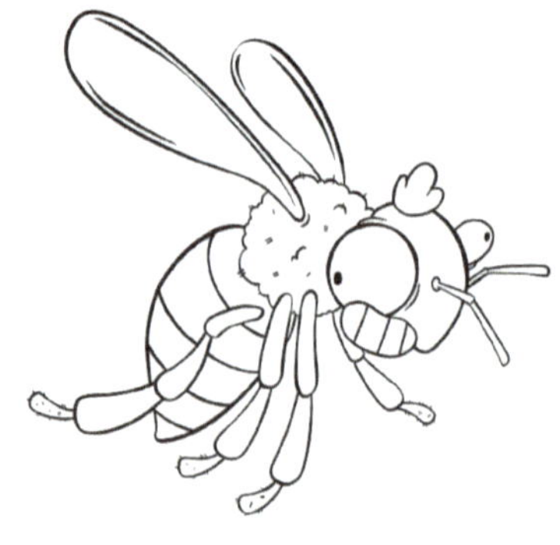

Honeybee

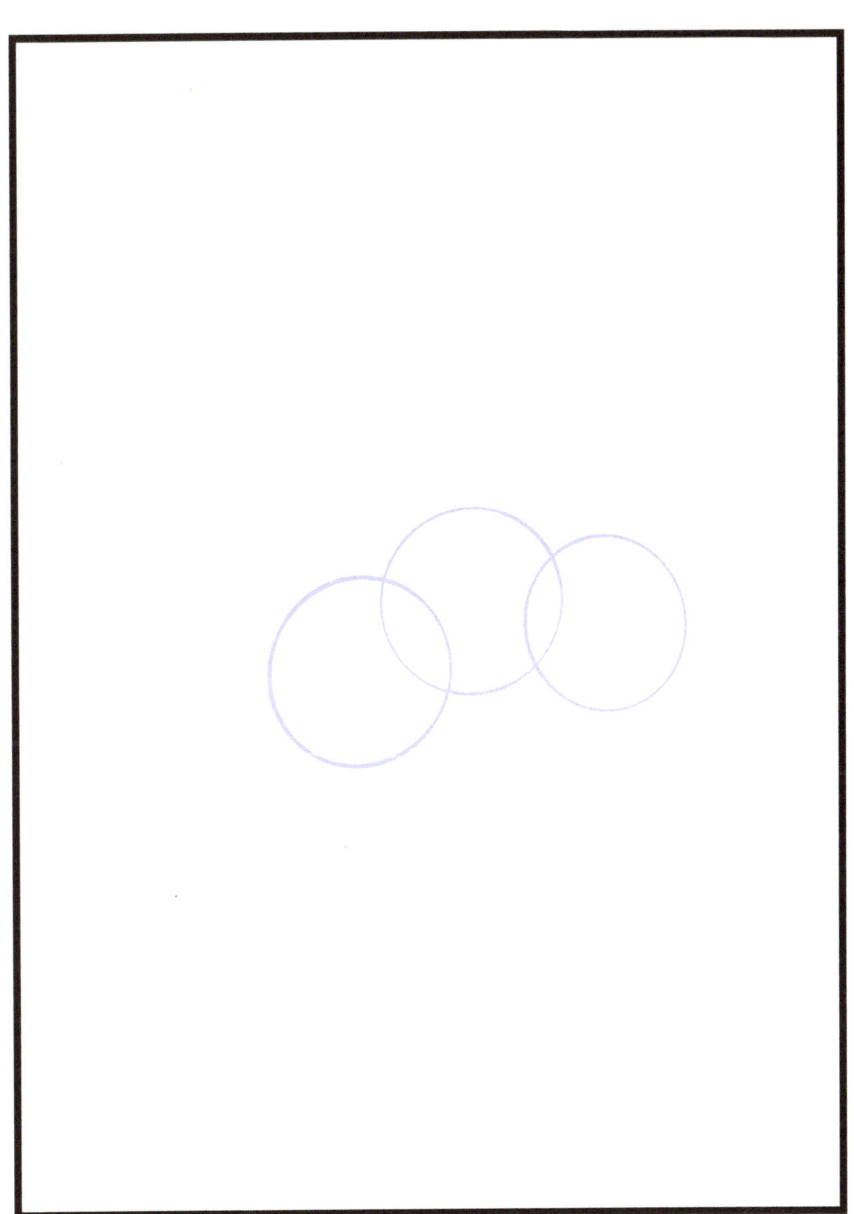

Turkey

1.

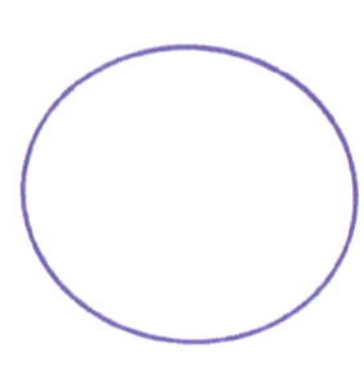

2.

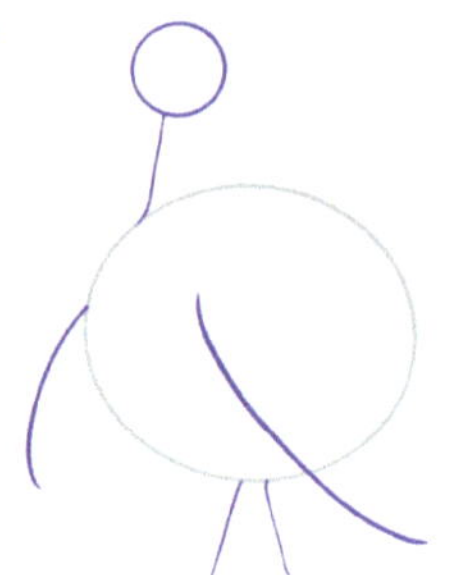

3.

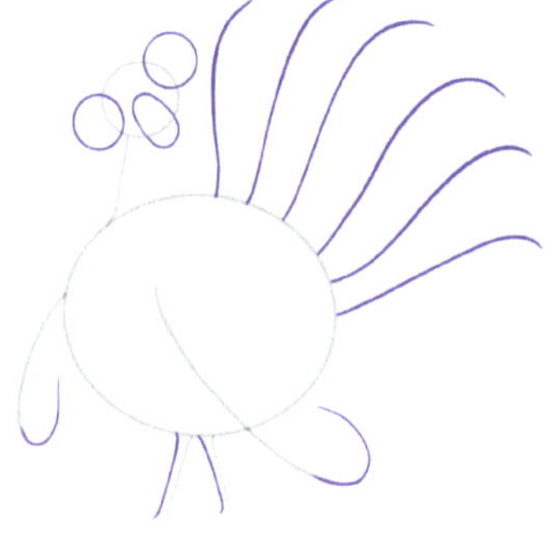

4.

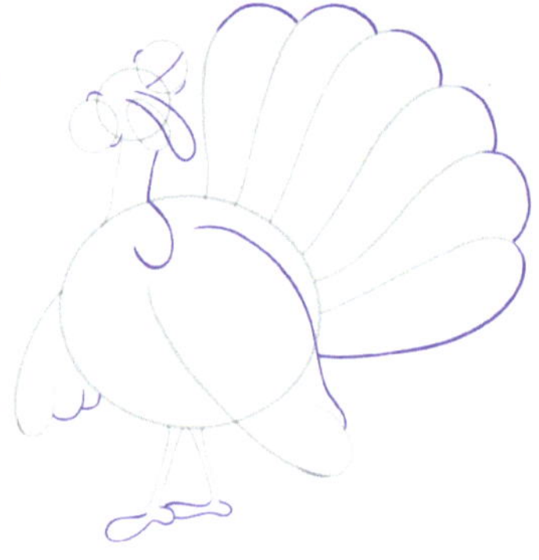

5.

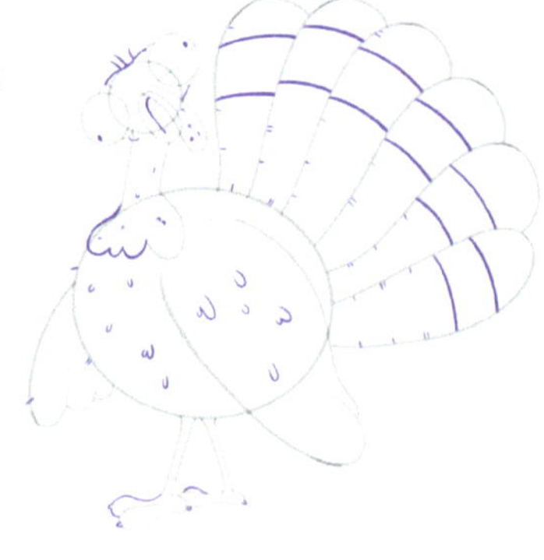

6.

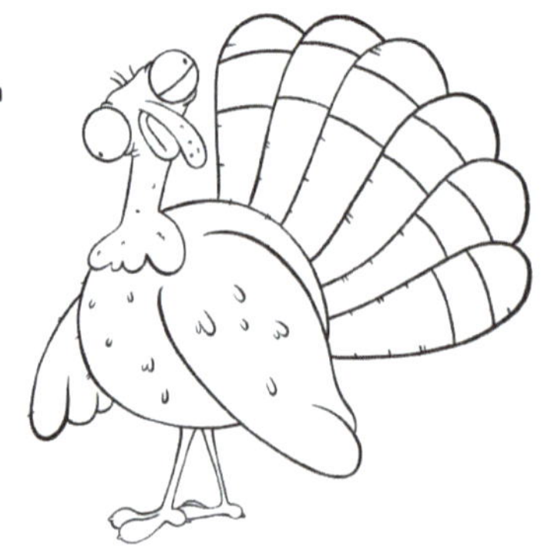

Turkey

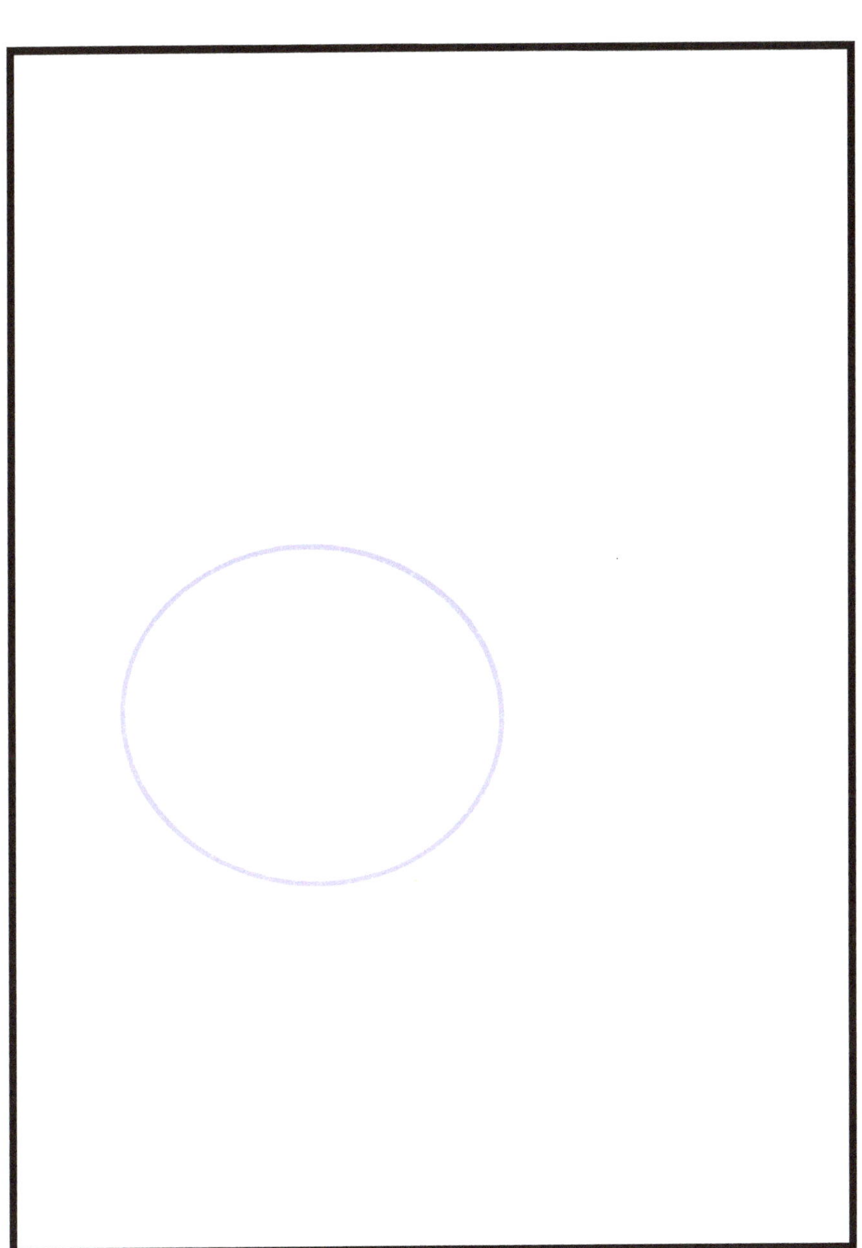

Buffalo

1.

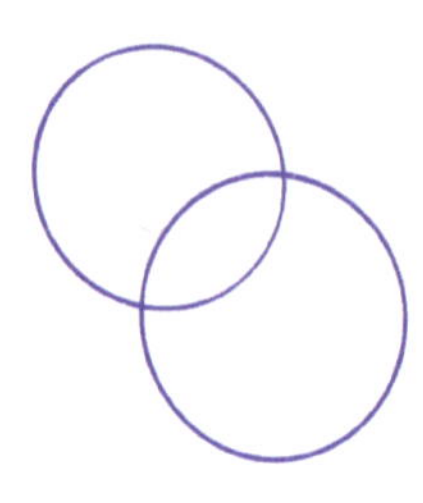

2.

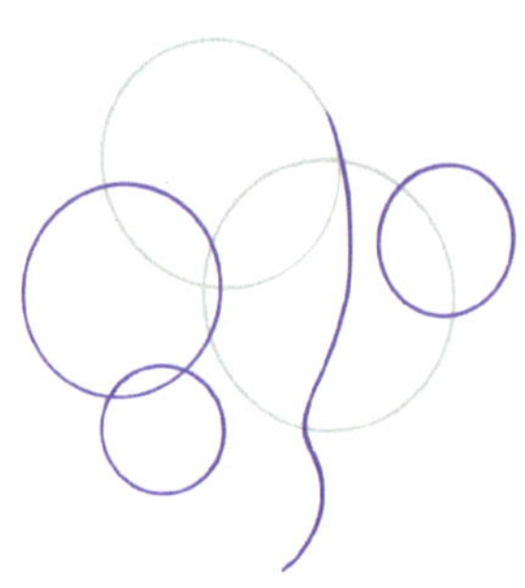

3.

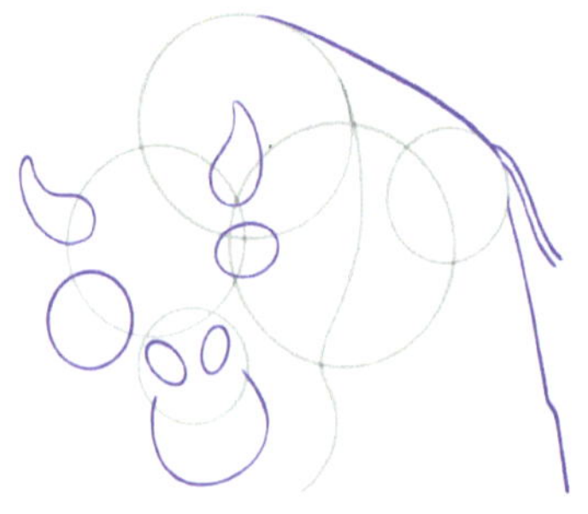

4.

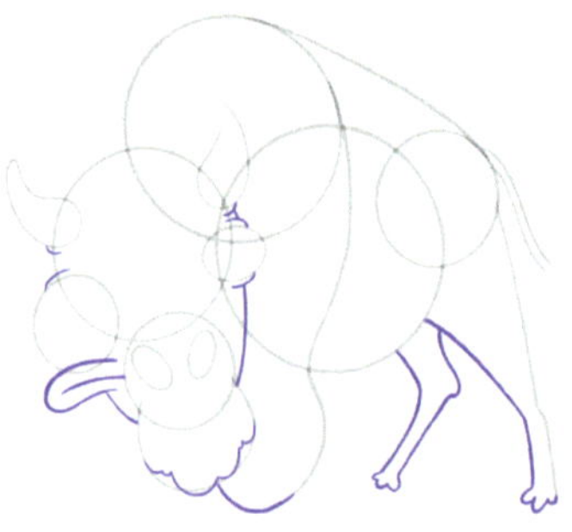

5.

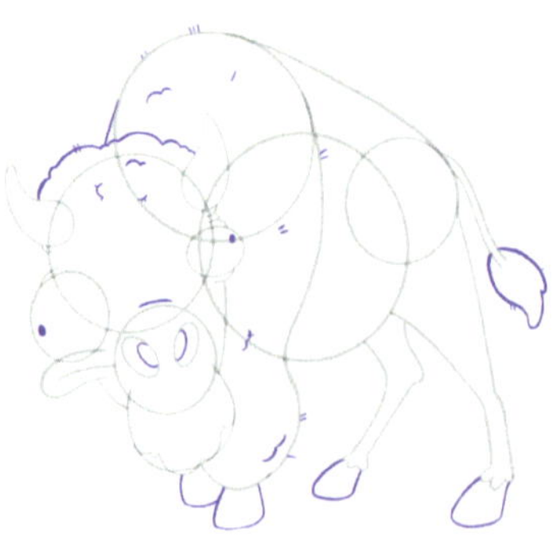

6.

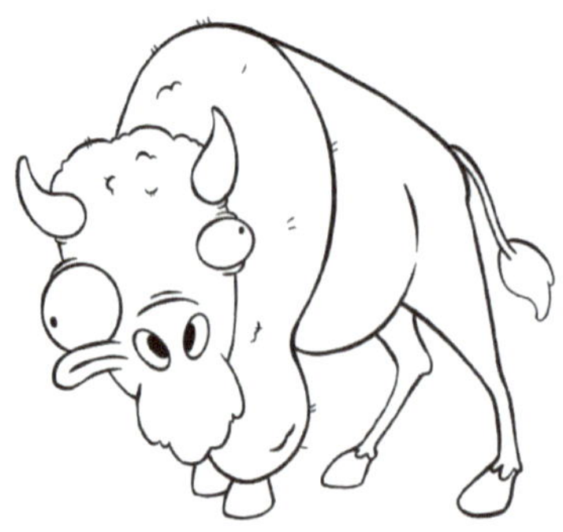

Buffalo

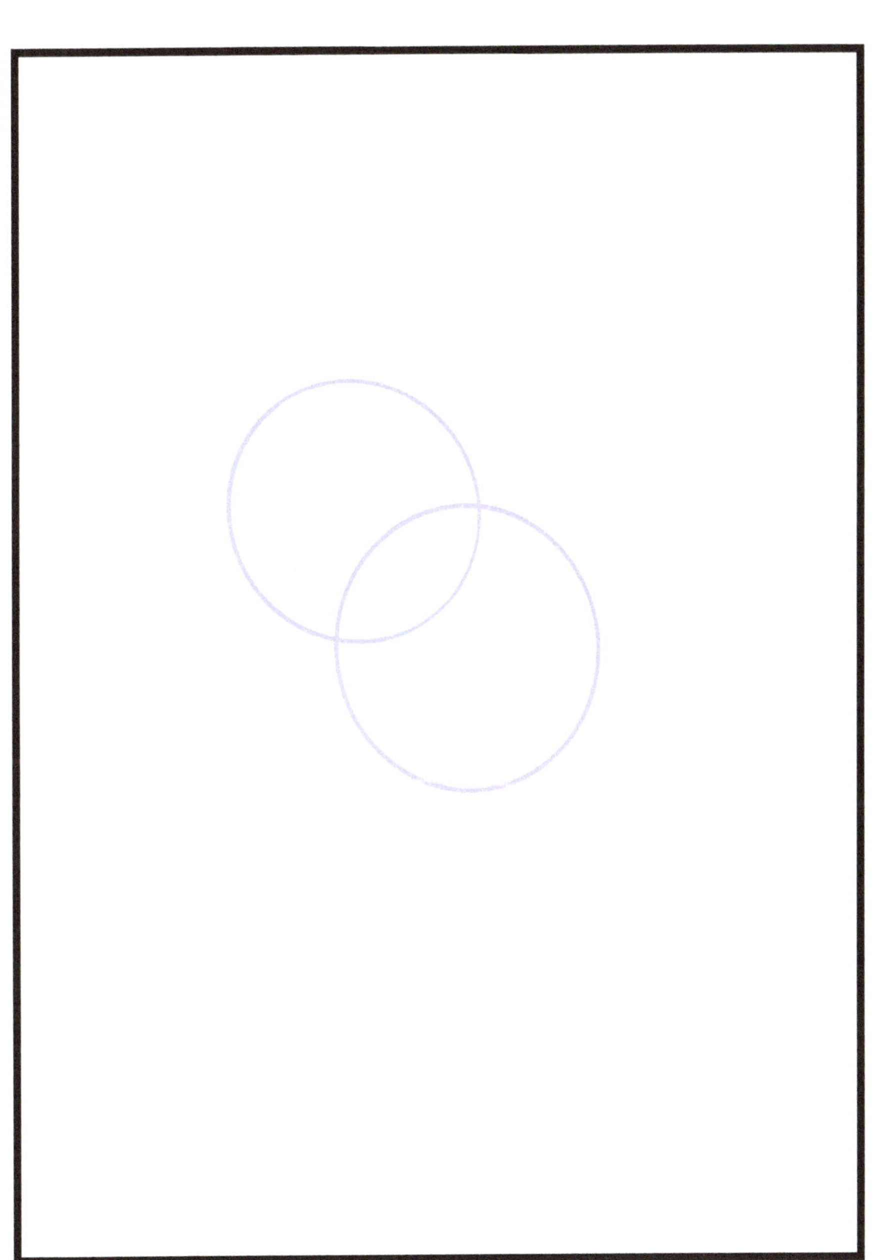

Ostrich

1.
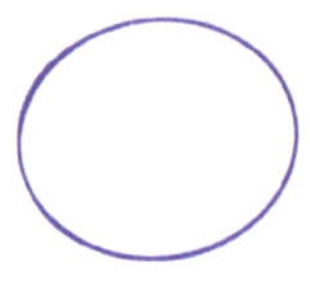

2.
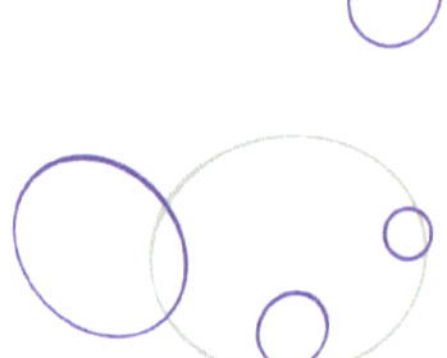

3.
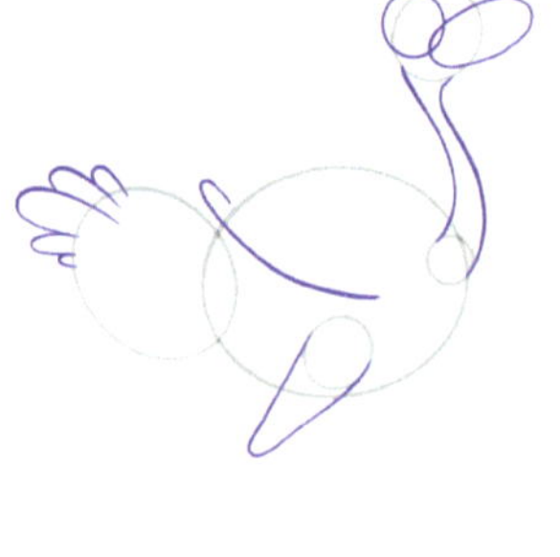

4.
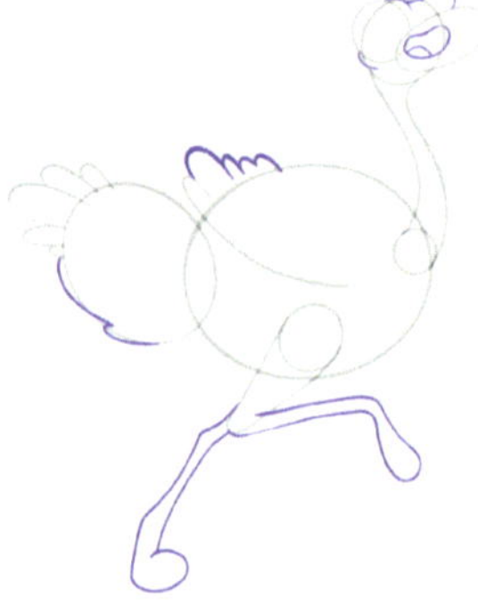

5.
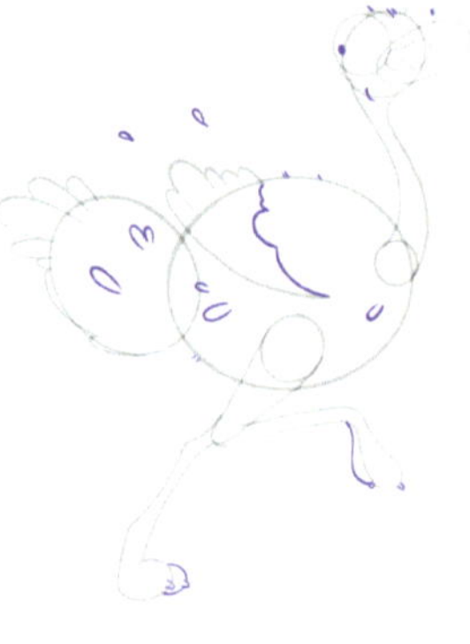

6.
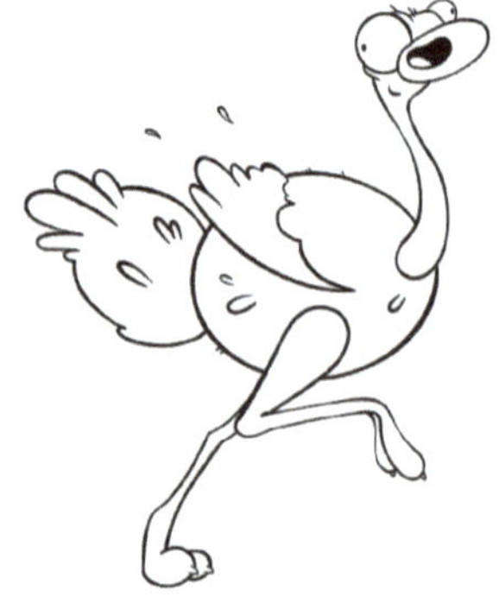

Ostrich

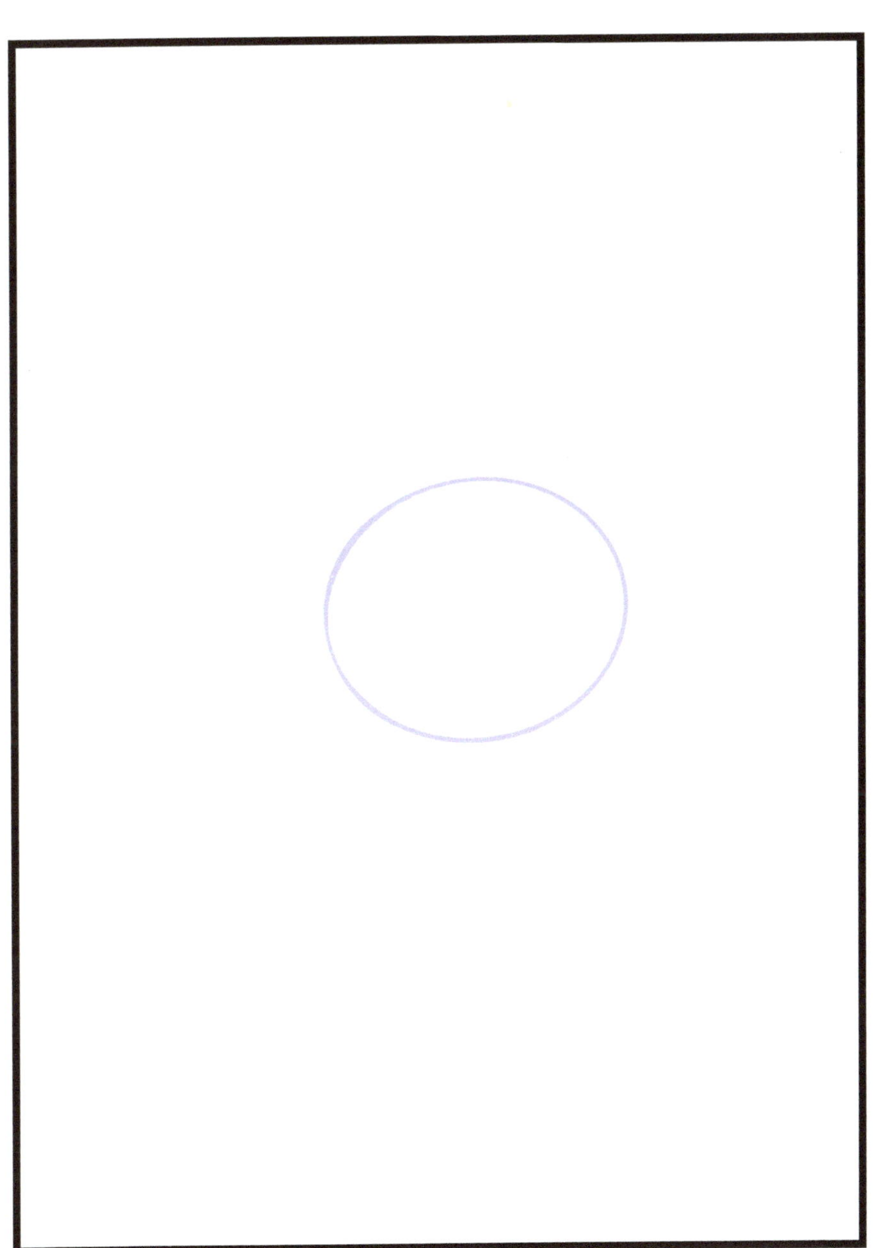

Ferret

1.
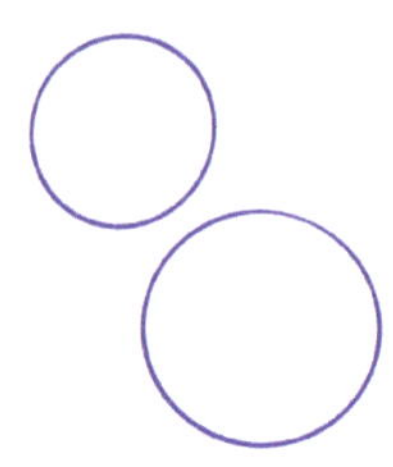

2.
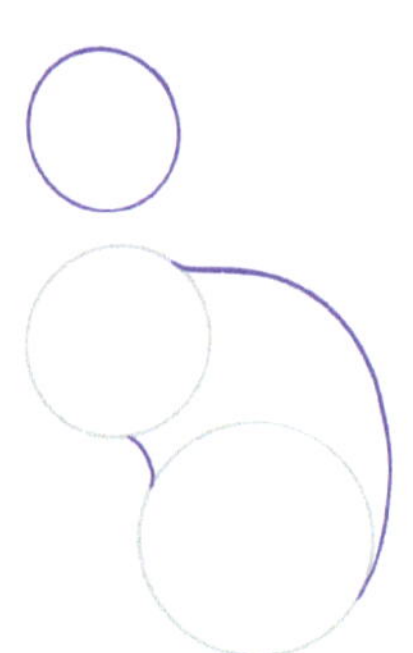

3.
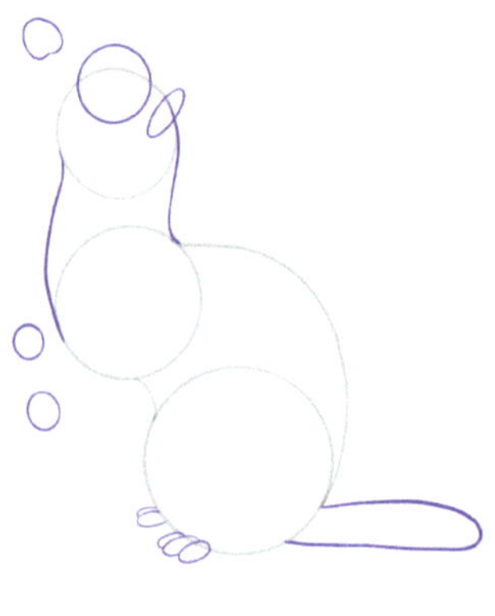

4.
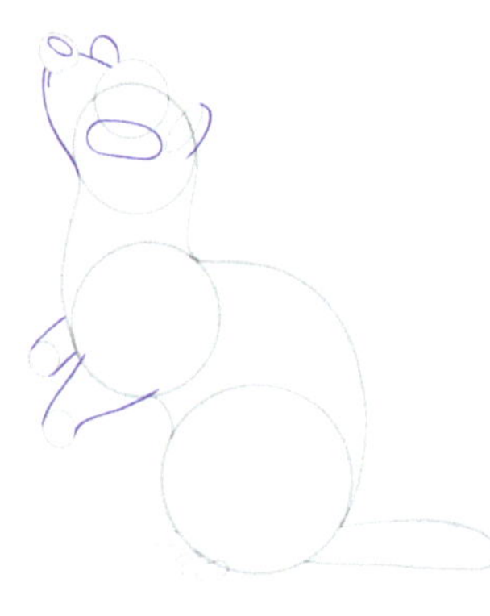

5.
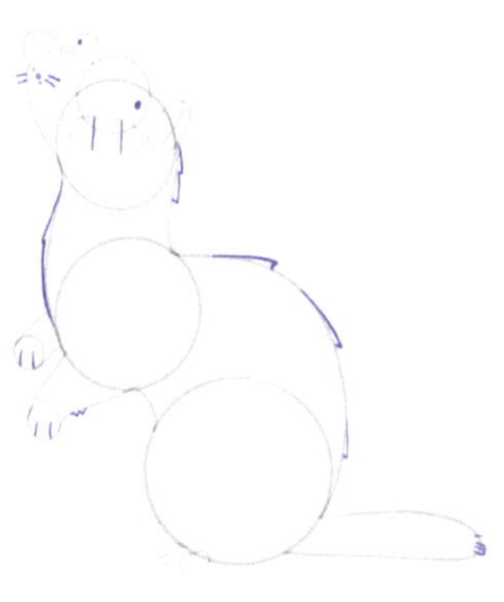

6.
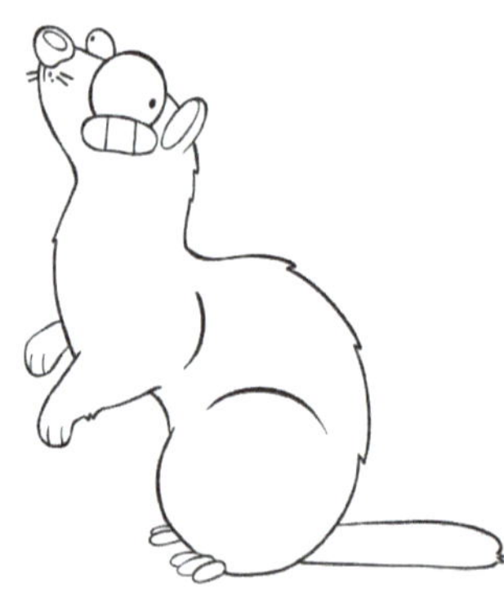

Ferret

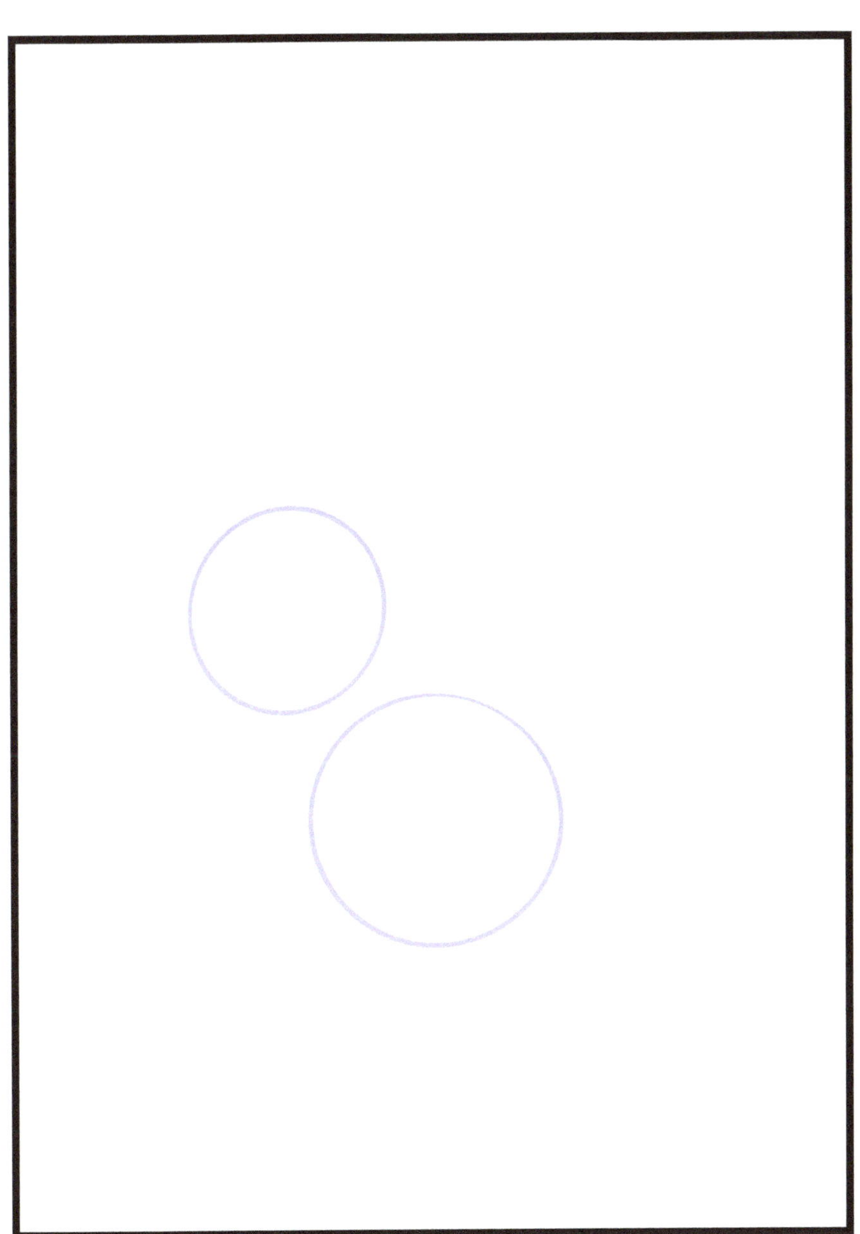

Sheep

1. 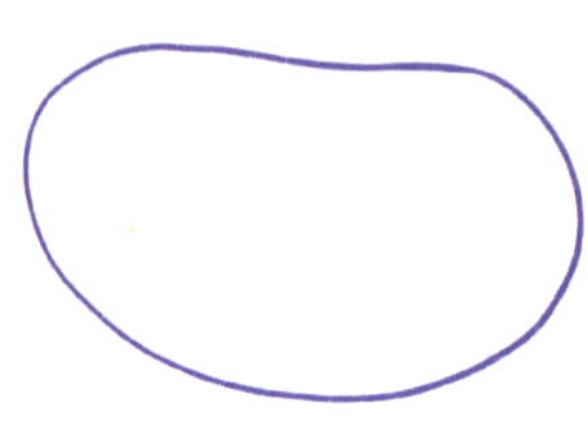

2. 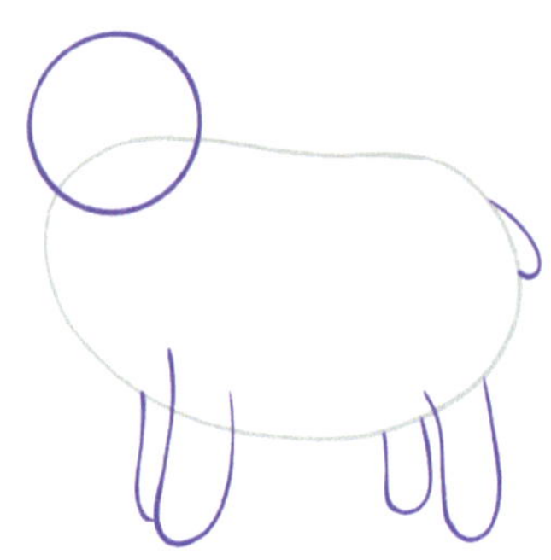

3. 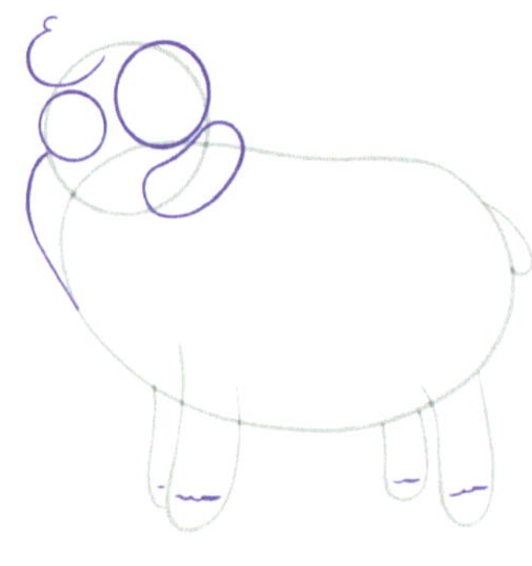

4. 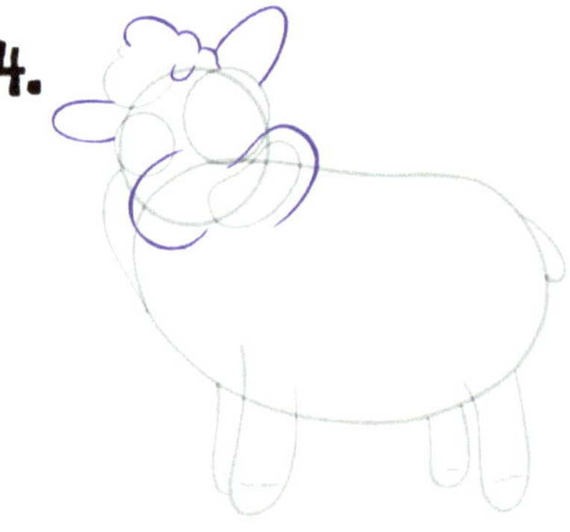

5. 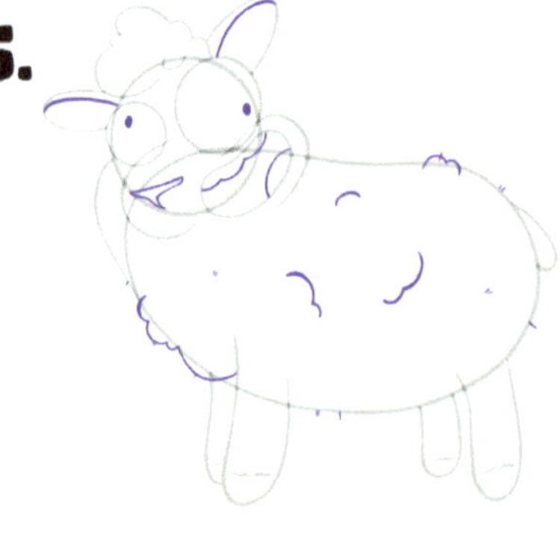

6. 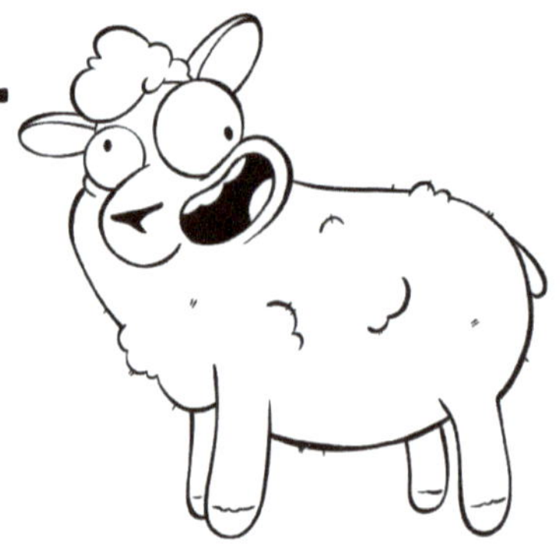

Sheep

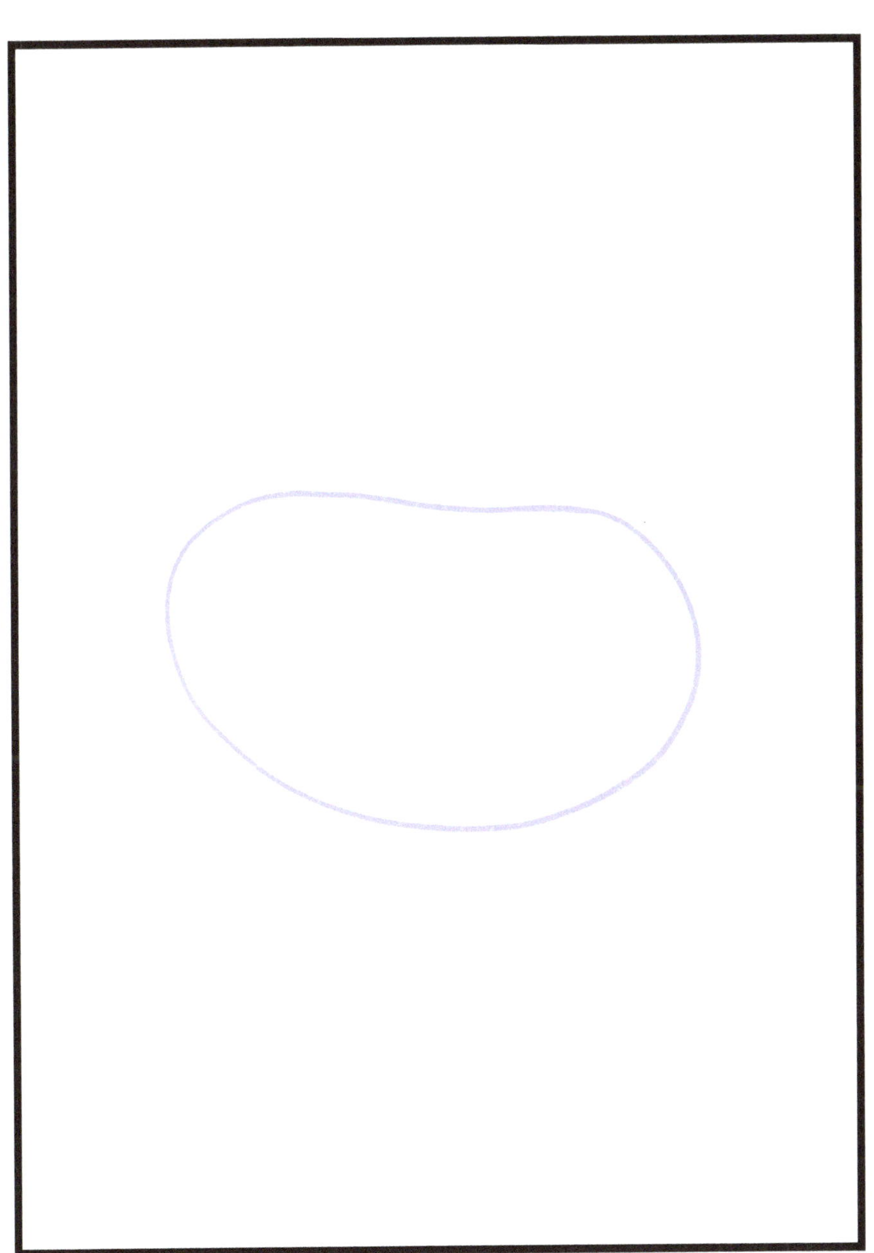

Lamb

1. 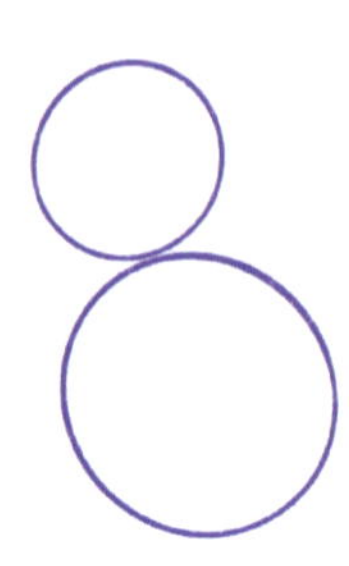

2. 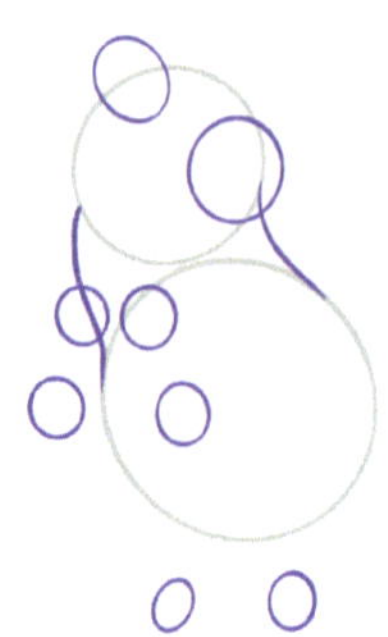

3. 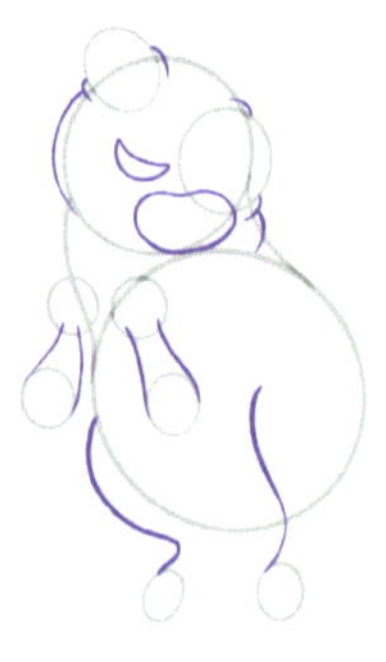

4. 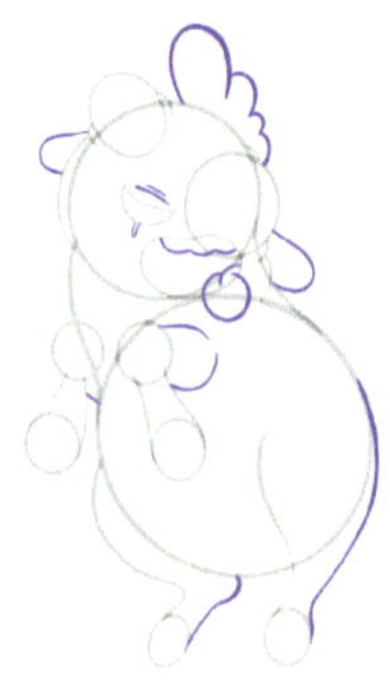

5. 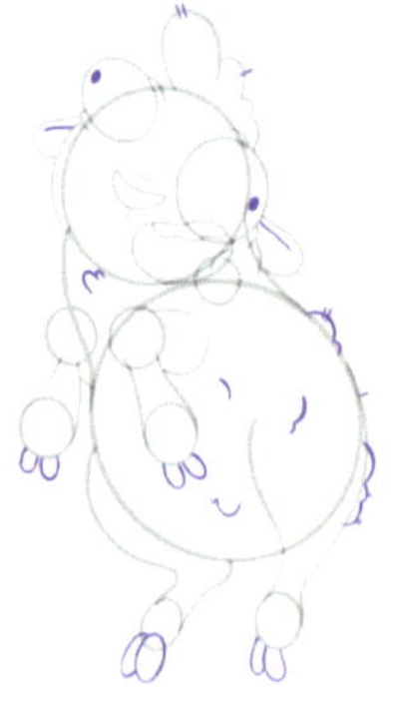

6. 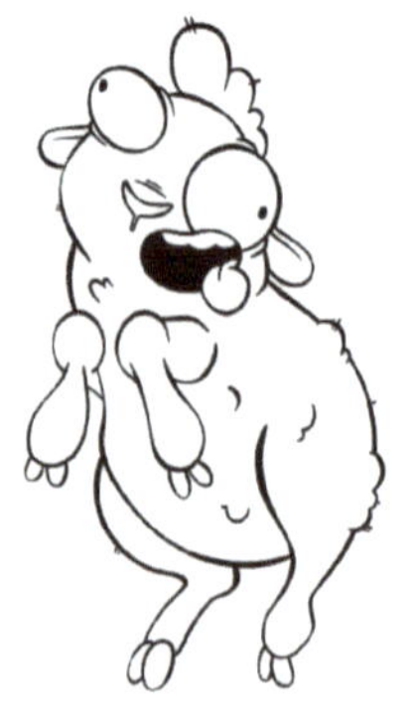

Lamb

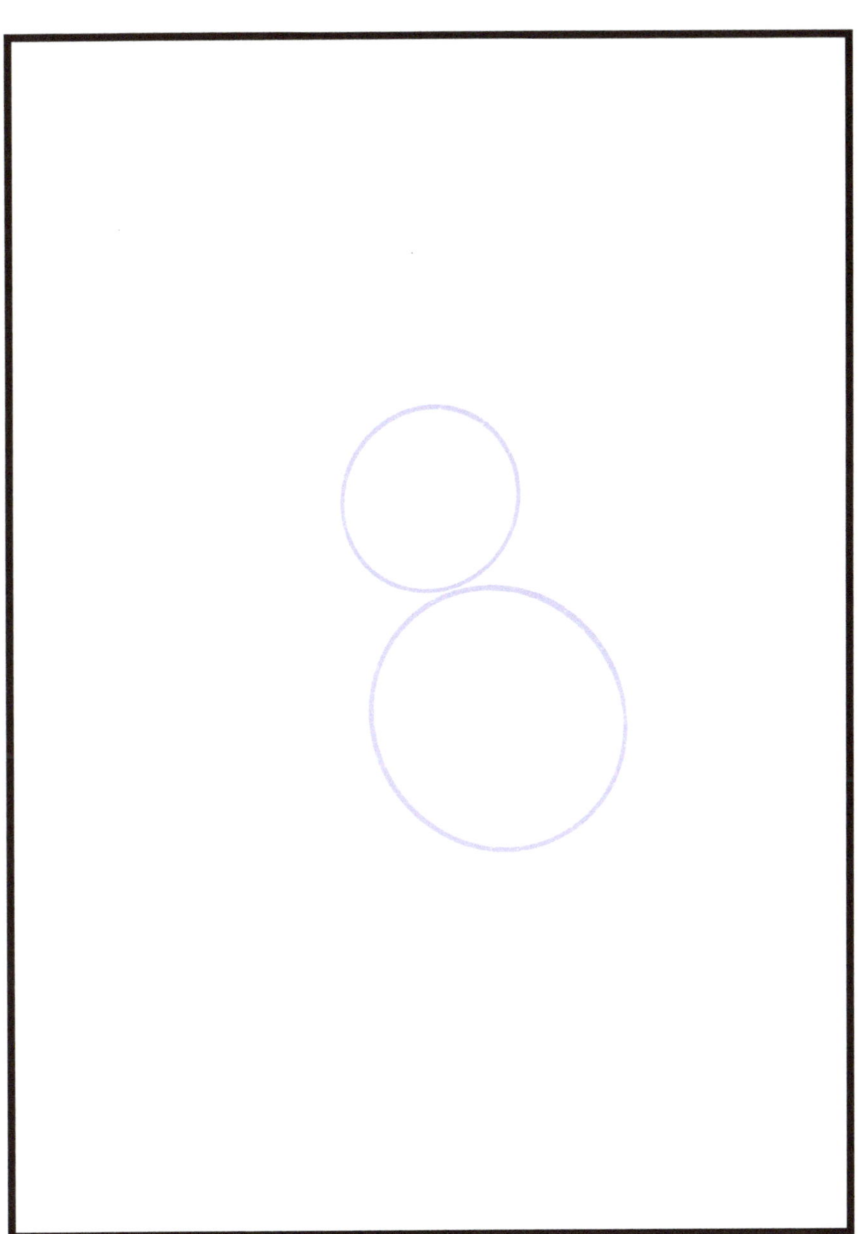